SUBJECTIVE ATLAS
OF PAKISTAN

Subjective Editions 2018

The moral rights of the authors have been asserted

First Edition published in 2018

Edited by Taqi Shaheen and Annelys de Vet

ISBN 978-9-08-291991-2

Printed in Belgium

SUBJECTIVE ATLAS OF PAKISTAN

Edited by
Taqi Shaheen & Annelys de Vet

CONTENTS

6 **Road to Zindabad**
Taqi Shaheen, Annelys de Vet

8 **A wing and many prayers**
Kamila Shamsie

16 **How to draw a map?**
Ayaz Jokhio

18 **Alternative maps of Pakistan**

20 **Pakistan according to Pakistan**
Samar Raza

30 **Cartographic lies**
Roohi Ahmad

32 **Mapodrama**
Hazique Zaheer

34 **Subtexts of Karachi**
Durriya Kazi

36 **City lines**
Wajid Ali Daharkiwala

40 **Liquid life**
Tahir Kayani

44 **Walking on the shoulders of Haramosh**
Mujtaba Ezaz

46 **High life**
Danial Shah

48 **Round around Karachi**
Nasim Ahmed

52 **A visit to my home town**
Aleem Dad Khan

54 **Roadside religion**
Zulfikar Ali Bhutto

60 **Domed legacies**
Farooq Soomro

64 **A brief history of Badshahi mosque**
Qasim Naeem

66 **Morirros's fossil**
Naiza Khan

68 **A guide to 'uncovered' Lyari**
Madiha Sikander

70 **A city emerges from a labor room**
Naila Mahmood

72 **Thy gentle head shall wear a crown**
Furqan Haider Bhatti

74 **Who do you want to be when you grow up?**
Madiha Sikander

78 **Brothers**
Malcolm Hutcheson

82 **Find the real Jinnah**
Imran Channa

84 **Sons of the soil**
Haroon Khan Wazir

88 **Grand miniatures**
Usman Saeed

90 **Cover girls**
Zainab Marvi

92 **Eyes on thighs**
Ahmed Ali Manganhar

94 **Covered in style**
Sarah Javed

96 **My wardrobe calendar**
Farrukh Afaq

98 **The new suit**
Monazza Fatima Naqvi

100 **All that glitters**
Zainab Nasir

104 **The legend of lotas**
Hafsa Macdi

106 **24-feet journey**
Rabeya Jalil

110 **Waiting to cross**
Sohail Zuberi

112 **Going through the roof**
Naseem Ahmad

114 **Weightlifters**
Furqan Haider Bhatti

116 **Mobile typographies**
Murtaza Ali

118 **Road suffering**
Ibrahim Yahya

120 **Street survivors**
Durriya Kazi

122 **Where the streets have no lights**
Arsalan Haneef

124 **Two-phone theory and
smart wallets of Karachi**
Rida Rohail, Onaissa Rizwani, Arsalan Haneef

126 **Lahoropoly**
Shumyle Haider, Maham Bosan

128 **Consumptional cart-o-graphies**
Sarah Javed

130 **The perfect go(a)l**
Nimra Saleem

132 **A guide to dhaba tea-drinking etiquette**
Sara Khan

134 **Watching you, watching me**
Naila Mahmood

138 **As seen on TV**
Sabin Agha

140 **News in use**
Alyna Farooqui

142 **From religious and corporate advertising
to political protests**
Rashid Rana

144 **Prohibited**
Mudasser Farooq

146 **Treasure chests**
Zaheer Chaudhry

148 **Welcome to the neighbourhood**
Risham Syed

152 **Street smart**
Sarah Javed

154 **Howzat!**
Aman Asif

156 **Alternate playing fields**
Furqan Haider Bhatti

158 **Diving into the unknown**
Nameera Ahmed

160 **Dao: the moves**
Zulfikar Ali Bhutto

162 **Hands up**
Tapu Javeri

166 **Divine conversations**
Arif Mahmood

170 **Make a wish**
Sana Khan Mamdot

172 **Jahaiz & Joseph Colony**
Malcolm Hutcheson

176 **Made in heaven**
Romano Karim Yusuf

178 **Desperate routes**
Khadim Ali, Raza Taj

180 **Articles of love**
Muhammad Hassan Miraj

182 **Relics of separation**
Sohail Zuberi, Omer Wasim

184 **Home away from home**
Madiha Sikander

186 **Faces of Partition**
Sara Hashmi

188 **For official use only**
Ahsan Jamal

190 **Border rituals**
Mahwish Chishti

192 **Mythological identities**
Adeela Suleman

194 **Alternative flags of Pakistan**

202 **Index of contributors**

207 **Credits**

208 **Subjective Atlas editions**

Road to Zindabad

What and who do we talk about when we speak of 'Pakistan' and the 'Pakistani' today? We posed this question to ourselves and more than sixty artists, designers, and other creative souls across Pakistan through a series of workshops and personal discussions. It invoked a new kind of thinking towards complex questions of identity through a criss-cross of unexpected alliances, conversational trajectories, and inspiring encounters. Together, with fresh perspectives, we set out to map the understanding of a country so often misunderstood.

The *Subjective Atlas of Pakistan* is the visual outcome of those encounters. Contributions arose from little anecdotes, trifles of everyday life, alternate symbols, and different points of view coming from implacable critics to the most passionate, romantic admirers. The atlas unfolds beyond linear terrains towards more nuanced insights. Through subjective mapping, it offers a humanized vision of ongoing conflicts pacified through visual poetics of personal experiences, everyday struggles, hopes and dreams, sufferings and sorrows.

The contributors have developed their own ways to dissolve worn-out clichéd patterns; their varying mediums created a constellation of possibilities to critically question the apparently objective. They mine deeper into the cultural complexities to find latent patterns within domestic and political situations, economic divisions, creeping social phenomenona around belief systems, ethnic and religious minority issues, and increasingly dominant immigration conflicts.

Using maps, inventories, photographs, and drawings, they investigated the microcosm of urban and rural lives through an open exploration. To reveal the complex realities, these explorations took us further into the traditions of nationalist rants, fictional propaganda, cultural identity wars either in the name of God, state or tourist-friendly pretentious soft-image, and corporate deceptions.

Some suggest it could perhaps be winds from the heavens that have kept Pakistan afloat in the whirlpool of religious extremism, natural calamities, and human misrule which continues to demand immense strength, resilience, and endurance from its people. There is also a realization that, to this end, neither overhyped nationalism nor naïve pragmatism offers any kind of substantial solution. If it did, it would have worked by now.

Perhaps, creative observers do not want to play the melodious songs of nationhood, however sweet they may sound. Sweetness doesn't offer security anyway. And neither do the visual authors of this book want to invest their destiny in a utopian country. Hence, the book transformed into a new proposition, a proposition of the irrigation of fresh artistic thoughts and ideas, which may possibly help to overcome local and global disorientation resulting from the casual promises of the state.

This atlas is meant to be a tool for an open dialogue in which creative observers become the most important players to construct parallel perspectives and fresh visions towards conflict resolution and a more peaceful society. As a humanist response to the complacency of power, it makes a modest non-violent attempt to cut through the noise of dangerously oversimplified media narratives and religious hate speech. It does so with an admission that its power to affect anything might be limited, but not ineffectual.

Let this atlas provide you an alternate view to measure and respond to the times we are living in. We hope this will sow seeds for yet more conversations and possibly help everyone safely navigate their way through the uphill road to Zindabad—the 'Land of the living'.

Taqi Shaheen is a Pakistani artist and documentary maker, Annelys de Vet is a Dutch designer and founder of *Subjective Atlas Editions*. Together, they initiated and edited the *Subjective Atlas of Pakistan*.

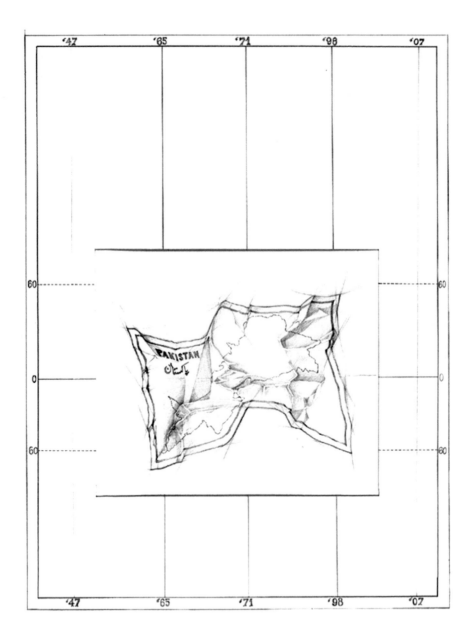

Marginal latitude
Roohi Ahmed

A wing and many prayers

Consider a pair of wings. They are separated by the width of a torso, to which each wing is anchored. Consider that this torso is both intimately known to the wings which sprung from it and yet, of late, their mortal enemy. A hostile body. The wings seek to claim they are entirely separate from the torso while indivisible from each other; and yet there is the fact of the connective tissue—half flesh, half feather—between each wing and the torso.

Of course the wings are East and West Pakistan; the torso is India. This is a map of the subcontinent at Partition, and from the very outset it announces itself as belonging to the realm of the imaginative, the metaphorical, rather than the literal. For how could it ever be a literal truth—this nation state which flouted the basic understanding of a nation state as being geographically contiguous? Only the imagination could hold such a state together—and the imagination failed entirely, which led to one wing un-pairing from the other, leaving behind a moth-eaten Pakistan. What is the sound of one wing flapping?

And so that nation of two wings, which required—and failed to achieve—a work of great imaginative sympathy to hold it together now required another, no less monumental task: to imagine itself anew less than 25 years after its first attempt at creating a myth of nationhood that could be sustained despite all the odds stacked against it. The originating myth of a nation created to safeguard the rights of one group (Muslim) from the domination of another group (Hindu) would have to be jettisoned after the massacres and brutality of 1971, which centred precisely around the issue of a less powerful group demanding more rights and being met with oppression. But what myth would take its place?

The obvious answer would be to create myth out of history in the way of most nations. Such a project should have been made easier by the reduced land mass of post-71 Pakistan, and no need to leap over the great breadth of India to bind all the parts of the nation into a single whole. And so the myth-makers of nationhood could have set about doing things in the tried and tested ways of nation state: focus on certain parts of history, airbrush others, amplify this strand, mute that one. What could have emerged from such a project would be a deep, broad, pluralistic history which would have among its high points the Indus Valley Civilization and the art of Gandhara.

But instead, in the existential angst that followed the creation of Bangladesh, a figure was brought centre stage, around whom the history of Pakistan could be told in a way that made it quite distinct from India and didn't require the participation of its former Eastern

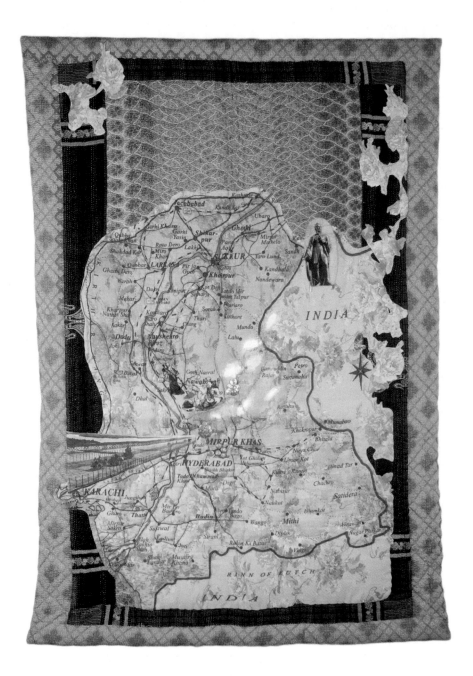

Sindh
Risham Syed

wing: this figure was Mohammad bin Qasim, the first Muslim general to capture territory in the Indian subcontinent—conveniently for the purposes of myth-making, that territory was in Sindh.

What this means is that when Pakistanis are taught their own history they are given to understand it is the story of Muslims in the territory that comprises Pakistan. In other words it's a history constructed in the overlap of Islam and territorial Pakistan; anything non-Muslim or outside-the-borders is almost entirely excised from history. In making Pakistan's history one that exists at the intersection of territory and religion, various and varied political leaders, religious groups, academics, and historians have created an ultimately unsustainable myth of a nation. The question: 'What kind of state is this?' has not been answered but amplified by the half and half way in which its history has been cobbled out of both religion and territory. Neither the Buddhist kingdoms of Gandhara nor the Muslim rule of the Delhi Sultanate can be part of this narrative (in fact, most of Mughal rule is also excluded—Shah Jahan only manages to enter history texts because of the monuments he built in Lahore).[1] What kind of state is this? One imagined by the unimaginative who fail to understand that any myth requires an internal logic, a thorough line of continuity.

Given the contortions, perverse imaginations, and flights of fancy that have gone into constructing the history and myths of the nation, is it any wonder that writers and artists from Pakistan so often return to the question 'What kind of state is this?', and attempt to find answers that don't strain credulity to the extent that the official narrative does. What those with power have poorly imagined, artists can better reimagine.

This isn't to say that all artists must directly take on the official narrative and seek to dismantle it. Every citizen or resident of a nation carries around their own stories, intensely personal ones, that may or may not interact with the official narratives. We also carry around our own obsessions and preoccupations, which may be the development of reverse swings in the history of Pakistan cricket or the different shades of green in a row of orchards or changing bus routes or pictorial representations of Madam Noor Jehan. The rewriting of history and changes of government and growth of one kind of political ideology and collapse of another may intersect with these stories and preoccupations—we may find a way as artists to make them intersect—but we also must insist on our own intimate relationship to the nation, and the freedom of our imagination to range over any aspect of life in that nation. As the Nobel laureate, Seamus Heaney said, 'Although they must feel answerable to the world they inhabit, poets, if they are to do their proper work, must also feel free.'[2] You could extend this thought (I do) to say that one of the ways of reimagining an official narrative is to speak and draw and sing and write of things that make up the unofficial story of a nation.

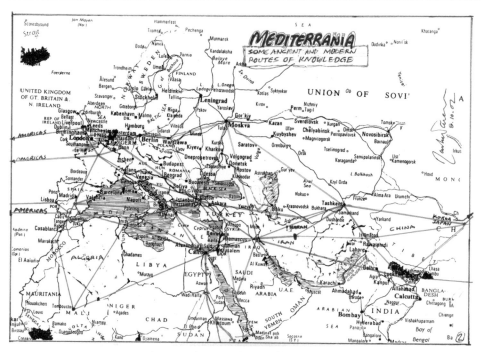

Ancient & modern roots/routes of knowledge
Rasheed Araeen

What better form in which to do that work of contesting the official and expressing the unofficial than in an atlas, which maps out the nation from a myriad of perspectives, producing images that sometimes complement and sometimes contrast with each other. Because these images don't try to wrestle themselves into a single overarching, ideologically driven narrative, they, ironically, work far more effectively as a whole than does the singular ideological narrative which has fissures where there should be points of connection.

It's worth recalling here that imaginative mapping returns cartography to its earliest roots. Ancient maps were used to illustrate stories, not to lead people from one place to another.[3] You would look at a map to be drawn deeper into the story of Ulysses making his ten-year voyage from Troy to Ithaca, not to work out how to make such a journey yourself in a more direct manner that avoids sirens and cyclops. It wasn't until Eratosthenes, the head librarian at Alexandria, set about mapping the world in the third century BC, that a distinction was made between scientific and literary mapping. In making that distinction, Eratosthenes removed Homer's writings from the corpus of cartography. Prior to that moment *The Odyssey* was considered to be as valid a source of map making as the accounts of travellers who had actually set sail to different parts of the world. To those of us in the

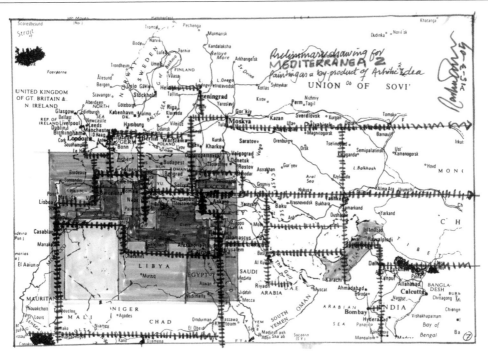

Artistic intreventions into physical borders through rail networks
Rasheed Araeen

twenty-first century, Eratosthenes' decision to exclude Homer and other storytellers from the realm of cartography seems like common sense. Yet it shook the foundation of cartography and remained a deeply contentious issue for generations. More than three centuries after Eratosthenes made that decision, Strabo, the author of the 17-volume *Geography*, remained deeply resentful of it and insisted that Homer depicted geographic truths in the language of poetry and so fully deserved his place alongside cartographers who drew maps based on their literal, rather than literary, travels.

And so—remembering that the Greeks are part of Pakistan's history, too, via Alexander the Great and the Indo-Greek kingdoms that followed—it is not a departure from the history of cartography but a return to it that can be found within this *Subjective Atlas* which uses illustration, narrative, imagination, emotion to map the nation, and to tell truths in the language of poetry (I say that with 'poetry' standing in for all art forms).

In addition to linking to the distant past, the forms of mapping within the *Subjective Atlas* capture something of the manner in which Pakistanis map the intimate spaces in which they live. Considerations of this intimate mapping have been something I've thought of and written about for almost twenty years now, since the day in Karachi when a friend's

Excerpt
Madiha Sikander

aunt, who had been living in New York for many years, asked for directions to someone's house. I started with '*You go down the hill by the graveyard near that really big house*' and she interrupted to ask why no one in Karachi could give you directions with reference to actual street names. Of course, it's an exaggeration to say no one ever does, but I started to pay attention after her comment to the ways in which Pakistanis guide each other around: '*It's the street leading to the Aga Khan hospital which has all those palm trees; turn when you come to the place where we had the accident with the donkey cart; keep going straight down the street until it's so deserted you think you've missed the house and just after you've reached that conclusion you'll see a white house on your right, and that's it*' and so on. Within such directions there are stories, and observations of what sets one thing apart from another, and humour, and a sense of shared space, shared reference points. Now that I've lived in London long enough to pick up other habits of how to get from one place to another, and also now that I am no longer in Karachi enough to be part of the shared reference points, I find myself relying on online maps for directions, but I still make a point of asking those who live in Karachi how to get where I'm planning to go. Not only because I want to hear them in order to feed my imagination, but because they can be useful in ways that go beyond online maps—*you don't want to go down this route because the traffic light stays red forever; at that corner there's a man who sells the best watermelons; there've been many robberies in that area so take a decoy phone etc.*

This book proves, that amid the official narratives imposed upon Pakistan, there remain these more intimate, unofficial, imaginative ways of knowledge. So here they are, the images of Pakistan by Pakistanis: the contours of the nation revealed as a dinosaur, the flag formed by a bowl overflowing with green chillies; Pakistan as Armystan, Pakistan as Prayeristan, Pakistan as A-Maze-ing Pakistan; here is the nation seen through its roadside temples and shrines and mosques, through the contents of its shopping trollies, through the variety and ubiquity of its headwear; here are its prayers in the form of clay lamps, its tangled routes through traffic. Here its faces, its stories, its celebrations. Here, weddings out of ashes. Here roti, here chai. Here eyes. Here thighs.

Kamila Shamsie is a writer, whose novels include *Kartography* and *Burnt Shadows*.

1. Asif, Manan Ahmed. *A Book of Conquest: The Chachnama and Muslim Origins in South Asia.* Harvard University Press, 2016. p. 177

2. *Staying Alive: Real Poems for Unreal Times*, ed Neil Astley. Miramax Books, 2003. p.295
3. Jacob, Christian. "Mapping in the Mind: The Earth from Ancient Alexandria" from Mappings, ed. Dennis Cosgrove. Reaction Books, 1999. pp 45-46.

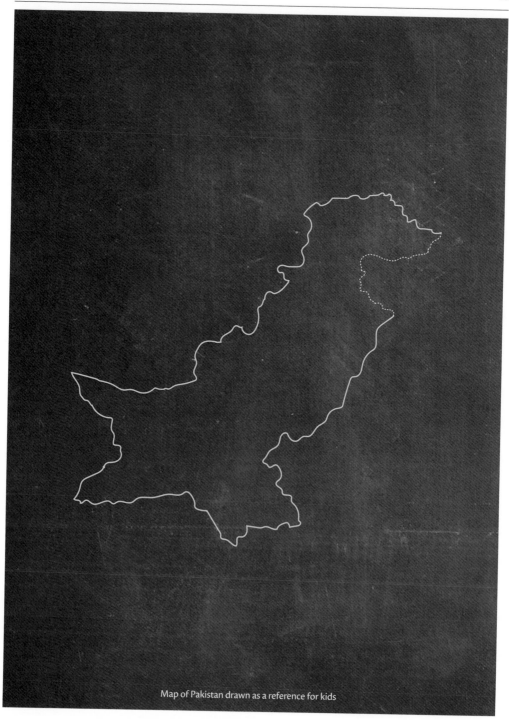

Map of Pakistan drawn as a reference for kids

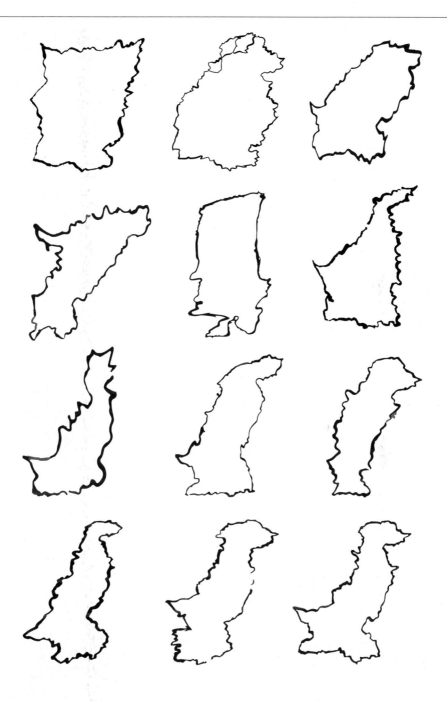

Maps of Pakistan drawn by children aged between 8 to 12 years,
who live in an informal settlement or *katchi abadi* close to Forman Christian College, Lahore.

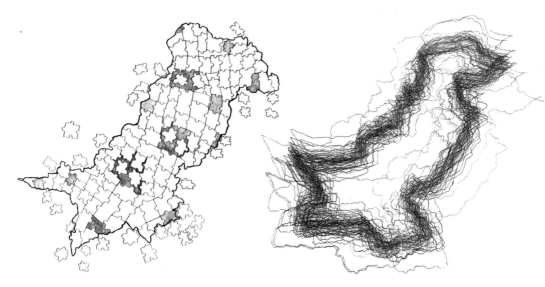

A game everyone plays and leaves
Chandan Baloch

An exercise in persistence
Roohi Ahmed

Borders exist only for the poor
Ayaz Jokhio

Accountability
Feica

MODI OR MOODY?

Greetings
Feica

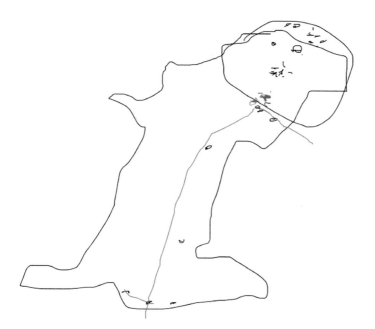

Mind zone

Chartar Park, Daman-e-Koh
Shakarparian
Pir Sohawa

Changa Manga
Murree, Nathiagali

Hyderabad

Peshawar

Naran, Kaghan, Swat,
Patriata, Atrot, Kalam

Hunza, Gilgit

China Border

Lahore

Rawalpindi/Islamabad

Goth Machi/ Bahawalpur

Sukkur

Jamshoro

Karachi

Mind zone
Rabeya Jalil

According to Balochistan province

**According to
Khyber Pakhtunkhwa province**

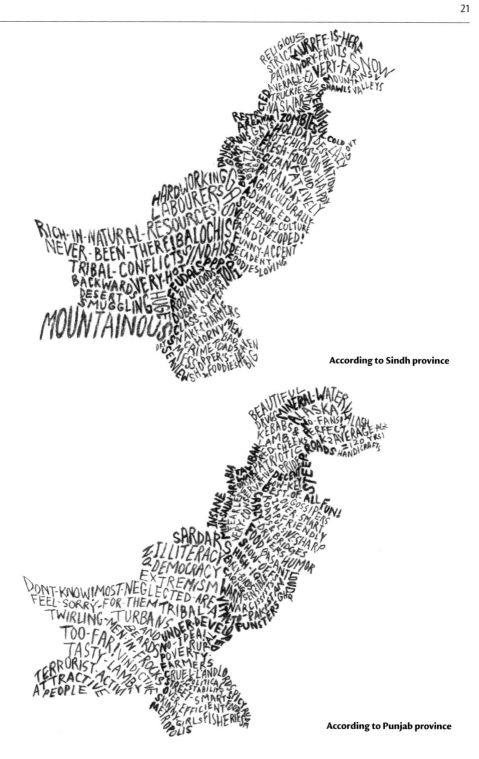

According to Sindh province

According to Punjab province

تمہارا بیٹا ہو۔
میرا اپنا گھر ہو۔
میری تنخواہ بڑھ جائے۔
آج سکول کی چھٹی ہو۔
گرمی کم ہو جائے۔
میری شادی ہو جائے۔
مجھے آئی فون مل جائے۔
تمھارے حق میں بہتر ہو۔
میں پانچ وقت کا نمازی بن جاؤں۔
لڑکے والے جلدی آ جائیں۔ بارش ہو جائے۔
میرے بال لمبے ہو جائیں۔ میں خوبصورت ہو جاؤں۔
تم ہمیشہ خوش رہو۔ تمہارا نصیب اچھا ہو۔
میرے میاں آ جائیں۔ میری مشکل آسان ہو جائے۔ میں پتلی ہو جاؤں۔
تمہاری عمر لمبی ہو۔ میں لمبی ہو جاؤں۔ میں پاس ہو جاؤں۔
تمھیں چاند سا دولہا ملے۔ میرا رنگ گورا ہو جائے۔
میری دعا قبول ہو جائے۔ میں حج پر جاؤں۔
میں پیرس جاؤں۔ میں ڈاکٹر بن جاؤں۔
میرا چشمہ ہٹ جائے۔ پاکستان جیت جائے۔
مجھے لڑکی مل جائے۔ مجھے نوکری مل جائے۔
میں پاس ہو جاؤں۔
میری باڈی بن جائے۔

A selection of frequently offered supplications to the Divine. People ask for sons, a house of their own, their husband to come home soon, a better salary and job, an iPhone, a fair complexion, less heat, to be thinner, become more religious, get married soon, a better fortune, longer hair, better height, a handsome groom, a trip to Paris, to become a doctor, to not need spectacles, more time off from school, a cricket victory for Pakistan, prayers to come true.

If God wills
Uroos Nazim

National instinct
Samar Raza

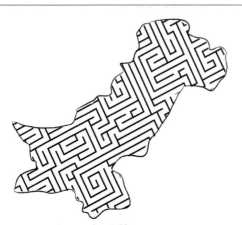

A-maze-ing Pakistan
Rida Rohail

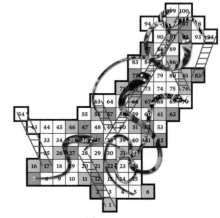

Play on
Mudasser Farooq

Generators and UPS
Ruhy Nasir

PACistan
Samar Raza

Prayeristan
Shumyle Haider

A dream of spring
Mir Sultan, Sana Ahmed Khan

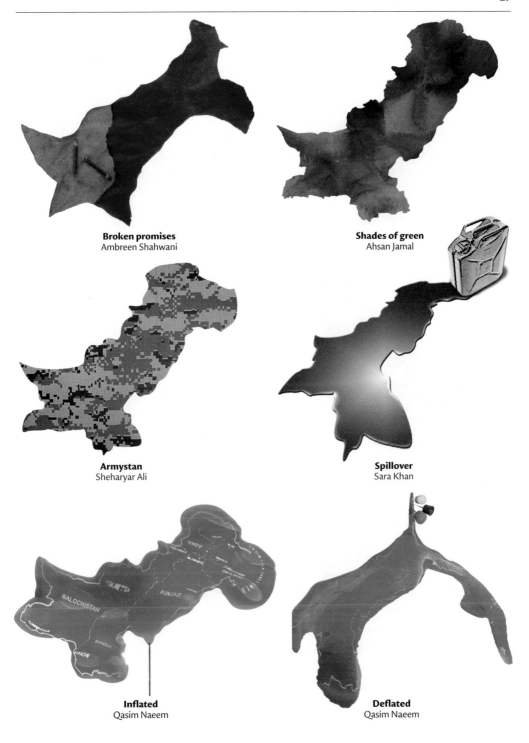

Broken promises
Ambreen Shahwani

Shades of green
Ahsan Jamal

Armystan
Sheharyar Ali

Spillover
Sara Khan

Inflated
Qasim Naeem

Deflated
Qasim Naeem

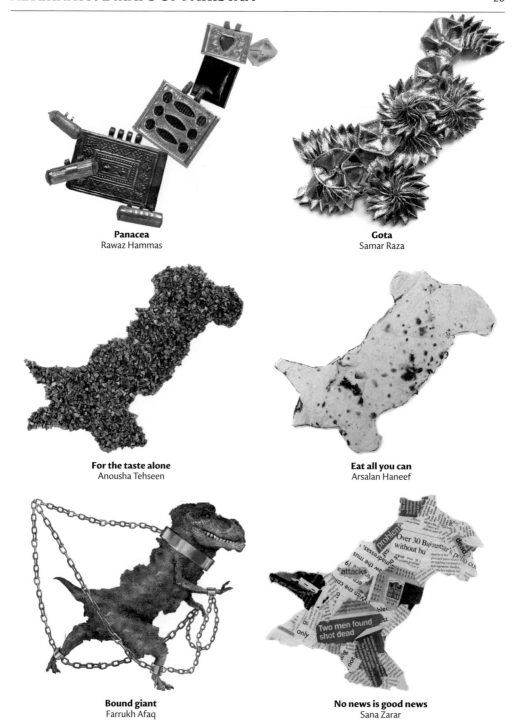

Panacea
Rawaz Hammas

Gota
Samar Raza

For the taste alone
Anousha Tehseen

Eat all you can
Arsalan Haneef

Bound giant
Farrukh Afaq

No news is good news
Sana Zarar

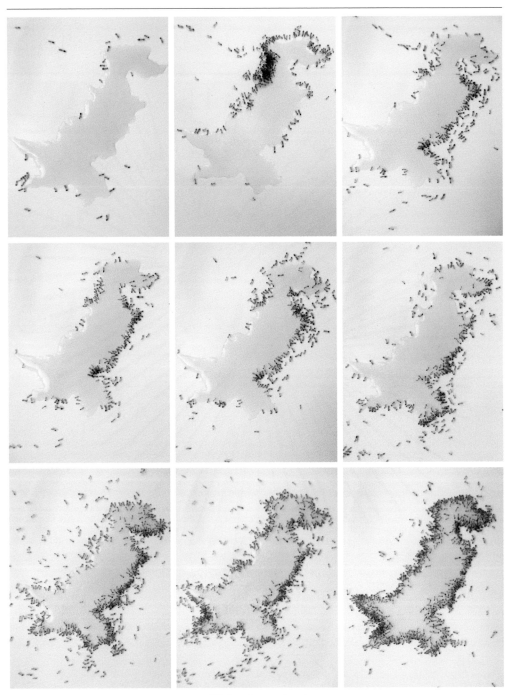

Hitting the sweet spot
Samar Raza

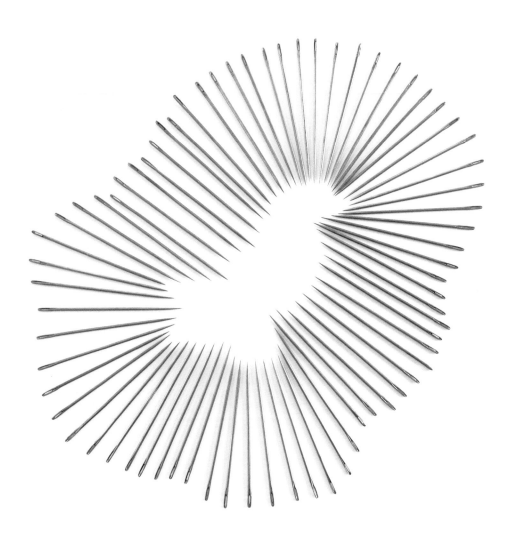

In the limelight
Roohi Ahmed

Crafted
Zulfikar Ali Bhutto

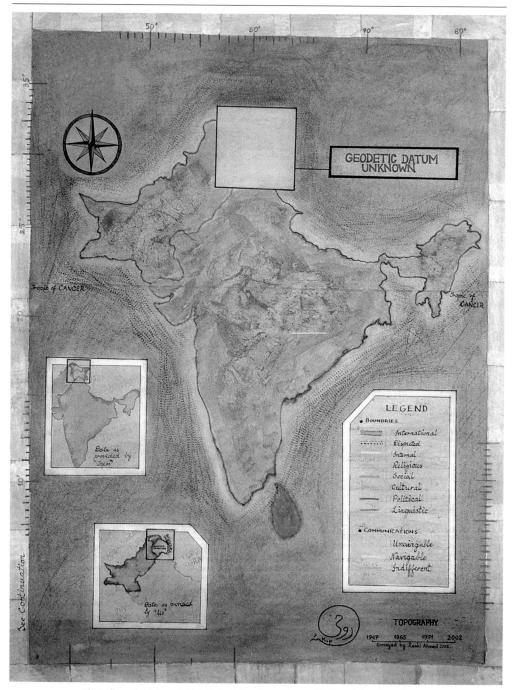

The Indian official stance is that Kashmir is an integral part of India and there is no dispute
whereas Kashmir is a disputed territory according to Pakistan's official stance.

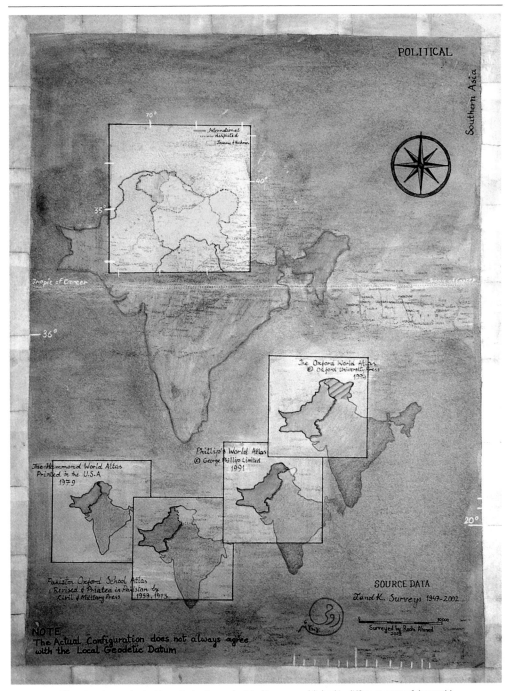

POLITICAL

Southern Asia

International
disputed
Jammu & Kashmir

70°

40°

35°

36°

Tropic of Cancer

Tropic of Cancer

The Oxford World Atlas
© Oxford University Press
1994

Phillip's World Atlas
© George Phillip Limited
1991

The Hammond World Atlas
Printed in the U.S.A
1979

20°

Pakistan Oxford School Atlas
Revised & Printed in Pakistan by
Civil & Military Press 1959, 1973

SOURCE DATA
J. and K. Surveys 1947-2002

0   50000

Surveyed by Rooh Ahmed
2002

NOTE
The Actual Configuration does not always agree
with the Local Geodetic Datum

These two images look at how Kashmir was depicted in maps published in different parts of the world.
They differ greatly from one another, making the ground reality elusive.

The way a country maintains its foreign relations exposes its needs, fears, hopes and political biases. These anthropomorphic maps go beyond geographical comparisons to offer one interpretation of Pakistan's relations with five frequently discussed countries.

America

England

China

India

Saudi Arabia

Durriya Kazi

SUBTEXTS OF KARACHI

Karachi is a secret shared by the people of Karachi. Here, maps are only used at the time of original plotting by the authorities or by the estate agents. People find their way through a complex yet efficient mapping based on locating shops or bazaars, large trees, missing manholes, broken walls, eccentric or famous houses, bus stops and so on. It is not necessary that these locations be very visually prominent. Popular usage creates fame or notoriety, which gives it a strange sort of immortality, occasionally the landmark, building, shop may have long since pulled down but continues a legendary life. These are extracts from my Meethapani project, in which people were invited to share their memories of locations in the city.

1. BUFFER ZONE
2. NORTH NAZIMABAD
3. MUSA COLONY
4. DAAK KHANA STOP
5. OLD GOLIMAR

Quratul Ain (24) BUFFER ZONE
Travelling to Buffer Zone from Gulshan-e-Iqbal, one crosses two bridges. I recognize
the first from the stench of the open drain it crosses and know I have entered Federal
B. Area, and when I smell the next I know I have entered Buffer Zone. My grandmother lives in Buffer Zone. I know where to turn by the old cars parked there. The
next landmark to her lane is a tethered donkey. Whether it is morning, afternoon or
evening, the donkey is always there.

Zakia (42) NORTH NAZIMABAD
The small houses in the narrow lanes of North Nazimabad in front of N block,
have more than six people living in a single room. In the same area there are large
residential plots of 1,000 square yards or more with large lawns and swimming
pools and more rooms than people. What a contrast! On the one hand are narrow
overpopulated lanes where you cannot hear anything above the noise, and on the
other side there is so much space and so few people that only silence reigns. Once we
did not get water for two weeks but I felt too awkward to ask the neighbours. Then
I remembered a tap placed outside a nearby house for people to slake their thirst
which had a sign *For the love of Allah*. It would be good to have these facilities all over
the city so people would not face the lack of a basic need.

Murtaza (22) NORTH NAZIMABAD
My house is in North Nazimabad. The area which lies between People's
Chowrangi and Sakhi Hasan is known as the D.C. Office area although the D.C.
Office has now changed into the City Government Union Office. The area left
of People's Chowrangi is Block M, North Nazimabad but is known by the Dental
College located there. A little further, bus passengers know the stop by the name
of a nearby house, Niaz Manzil. There is a crossing just beyond known as Landi
Kotal Chowrangi or Thieves Chowrangi. I don't know the story behind this
name, but the Taimuria Police Station is located there. Maybe that's why it is
called Thieves Chowrangi.

Zohaib (20) MUSA COLONY
The localities in the area where I live have lovely names whether they are nice or not.
Mujahid Colony, Musa Colony, Kali Basti, Pak Sarhad Colony or Khando Goth are
worth mentioning. Each has its own character. Mujahid Colony began for Afghan
refugees after the Soviet invasion. Today the residents are labourers, rickshaw and
taxi drivers. Alcoholic beverages are sold openly in Kali Basti. Thugs and gangsters
live here. Musa Colony has a big centre for hashish with the protection of the police.
There is also a big spice market here and Karachi's largest recycling market. Glass,
plastic and paper are sorted here and sent on. Pak Mujahid Colony was established
for poor labourers but as fortunes grew, they have built their own shops.

Neelum (33) DAKHANA STOP
This is the stop from which one street goes to Teen Hatti, one towards Sindhi Hotel,
one towards Nairang cinema, and one towards Nazimabad. A little ahead is Bismillah
Bakery and a few lanes down is my house. I have lived here for 25 years. As soon as
I could understand, I witnessed political turmoil, lawlessness and the absence of
values. People casually take to the streets to stone cars, burn houses or participate
in gun battles. The strange thing is that if you ask the Shia protestors what the dif-
ference is between Shias and Sunnis, they probably would not be able to tell you.
Those kids who stone police vehicles have no idea why they are doing it. Perhaps, it is
simply fun for them. I have always noticed that the ones who throw stones or shoot
at people are never themselves stoned or shot at. It is always an innocent person who
has no idea why he was attacked!

Mama (33) OLD GOLIMAR
Old Golimar is a historic area. Its population is 70,000. I was born there and grew up
in the area known as Noor Muhammad Village. I run a free education centre.
I love this locality, maybe because I was born here. I love the strong tea at Munshi
Hotel and the daal fry of Noorani Baloch Hotel is delicious. Everyone appreciates the
simplicity and passion of the people of this area. I especially love the image when
labourers, tired after a hard day's work return from factories and fill the road from
end to end.

Drawn during my journeys across Pakistan

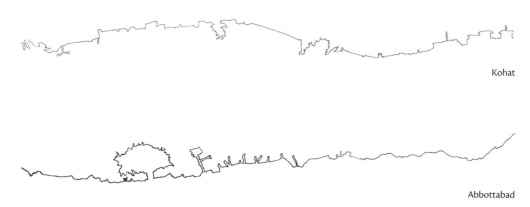

Kohat

Abbottabad

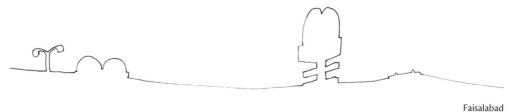

Faisalabad

Athmaqam, Neelam Valley

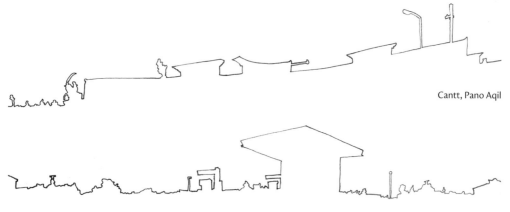

Cantt, Pano Aqil

Daharki GT Road Fuel Station

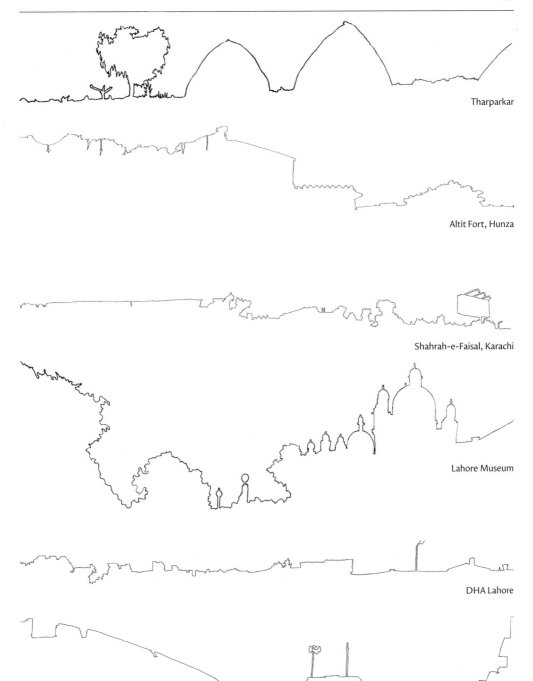

Tharparkar

Altit Fort, Hunza

Shahrah-e-Faisal, Karachi

Lahore Museum

DHA Lahore

Gwadar

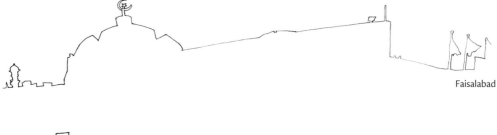

Faisalabad

Old Lahore

Daharki Engro Plant

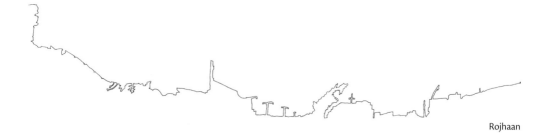

Mirpur Mathelo, GT Road

Rojhaan

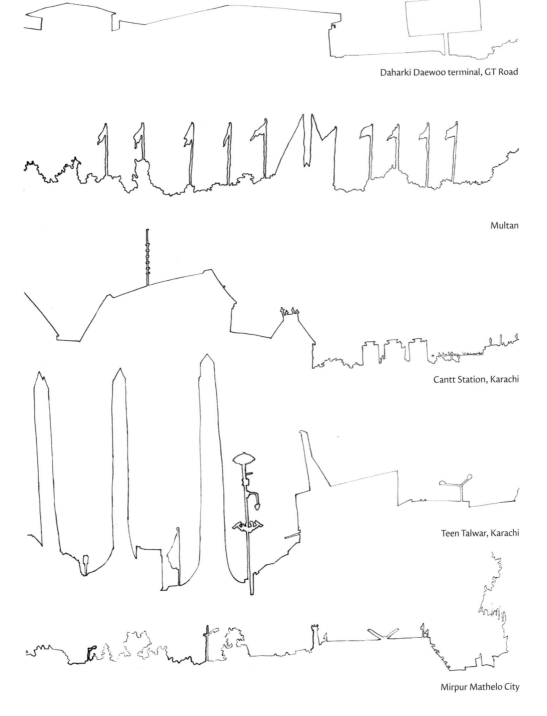

Daharki Daewoo terminal, GT Road

Multan

Cantt Station, Karachi

Teen Talwar, Karachi

Mirpur Mathelo City

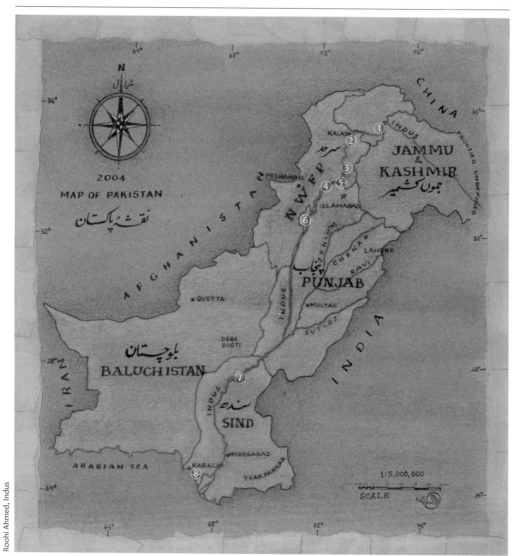

Flying for over 20 years, across and along the Indus River, I have always been humbled by its might. It always has something new to intrigue. In the northern highlands, it is the master carver that gorges along Nanga Parbat (15,000 to 17,000 ft deep). Indus, the longest river of Pakistan, originates in the western part of Tibet. In Kashmir it crosses the United Nations ceasefire line and, in Baltistan district, enters Pakistan-Administered Kashmir. From here on it is Pakistan's river; Pakistan's first town on the upper Indus, Skardu, at 7,500 feet above sea-level, stands on a bluff near the junction of the Indus and one of its great right-bank tributaries, the Shigar. Indus flows through Gilgit-Baltistan, and Khyber Pakhtunkhwa*, and then runs along the entire length of Punjab province to merge into the Arabian Sea near the port city of Karachi in Sindh province. **

*   NWFP was renamed Khyber Pakhtunkhwa in 2010
** The word 'Indus' is the romanised form of the ancient Greek word
    'Indós', borrowed from the old Persian word 'Hinduš' which in turn
    was borrowed from the Sanskrit word 'Sindhu' which means stream

1 Skardu, Gilgit-Balitistan	3 Haripur, Khyber Pukhtunkhwa
2 Thakot, Khyber Pakhtunkhwa	4 Khushal Khan Bridge, KP & Punjab

5   Ghazi Tabela Dam, Khyber Pakhtunkhwa

6   Mianwali, Punjab

7

Sukkur, Sindh

8

Karachi, Sindh

Haramosh La (5,100 m) lies on the shoulder of Mt Haramosh, Rakaposhi-Haramosh range (sub range of the Karakoram). It connects Haramosh valley of Gilgit region with Shigar valley of Baltistan. Haramosh La is considered as one of the toughest among high altitude passes in Gilgit-Baltistan. The passing is enclosed by Laila (6,986 m) which towers over the juncture of the Haramosh and Chogolungma Glacier, Mani (6,685 m) and Haramosh peaks (7,409 m). It is one of the most formidable trekking routes in the Karakoram.

Mani Peak (6,685 m)

Mount Haramosh (7,406 m)

Day 1 Started a 2 hour trek from Iskere at 4:40 p.m. to camp at first village of Kutwal
Day 2 Spent second night at advance basecamp 3,800 m (little higher than the actual base camp) of Haramosh La
Day 3 Started our climb at 4:00 a.m. and summit the La around 1:45 p.m., the last 100 metres were near an 80-degree angle
Day 4 6 hour trek to camp at the foot of Laila Peak
Day 5 Started around 8:00 a.m. and did long stretch along Chogolungma glacier to reach Arandu at 7:15 p.m.

Shandoor *top*
3,586 m | 21/09/2014 | 4:24 p.m.

Shandoor *top*
3,720 m | 05/06/2015 | 2:10 p.m.

Babusar *top*
4,355 m | 12:48 | 11/09/2011 | 12:47 p.m.

Ziarat
3,010 m | 07/06/2010 | 10:42 a.m.

Deosai
4,260 m | 26/07/2015 | 7:57 a.m.

Phandar lake, Ghizer
2,969 m | 4/06/2015 | 7:26 p.m.

Kalapani, Deosai
3,673 m | 01/10/2014 | 1:48 p.m.

Sheosar lake, Deosai
3,947 m | 01/10/2014 | 12:20 p.m.

Kuragh, Chitral
2,048 m | 07/06/2015 | 6:04 p.m.

Quetta
2,048 m | 07/06/2015 | 6:04 p.m.

Indus river, Skardu
2,264 m | 30/07/2015 | 7:05 p.m.

Chowkandi graveyard, Karachi
1 m | 29/10/2015 | 12:06 p.m.

Ziauddin Chowrangi

Native Jetty Bridge

While living in Lahore, I had always dreamt of going back to my home town on the slowest possible drive. These images chronicle my 996 km journey from Lahore to Hunza on a heavyweight truck which took me an exhuasting three days.

On the new road built by China, as its One-Road, One-Belt initiative with Pakistan, I realized that the roads are always constructed for the trucks and traders, without whom there will be no roads.

When colonial traveller and spy, Richard F. Burton, travelled through the province of Sindh via the River Indus he was taken by the immense amount of shrines—both large and small— that dotted the countryside. Very little has changed since the 1850. Mosques, Hindu temples and shrines of varying sizes, some only big enough to fit a handful of worshippers, continue to dot the land. They are simple structures, a room of solitude for weary travellers in need of faith, village residents wanting a space of solitude or for those lost and in need of direction. In a nation fraught with sectarian violence they have become precious evidence of a tolerant landscape.

Temple, Matiari

Temple, Umarkot

Temple, Adhe jo Tar

Temple, Sukhpur Qabr

Temple, Umarkot

Temple, Mirpukhaas

Temple, Anwar Jat

Temple, Kaasbo Shiv

Temple, Kaasbo, Chamunda Mata

Temple, Sukhpur Mata

Temple, Sardharo

Shrine, Mahotta

Shrine, Mitiari

Mosque, Mehr

Mosque, Rehm Ali

Mosque, Goth Miandad Khoso, near Jamshoro

Mosque, Surango

Mosque, Kantio

Mosque, Dodai, Larkana

Mosque, Jamshoro

Church, Larkana

Shrine, Moro Bypass

Shrine, Sehwan

Temple, Sakari

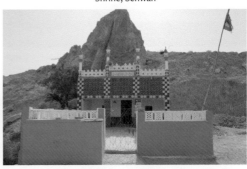

Mosque, Sehwan

Shrine, Rehm Ali

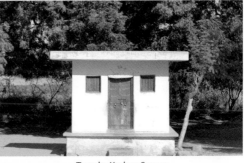

Temple, Kasboo Square

Temple, Nagarparkar

Temple, Matiari

Temple, Kaasbo

Shrine, Khwaja Khizr

Mosque, Kehro

Mosque, Achu Kohli

Temple, Sadhu Bella, Sukkur

Mosque, Kacha, Khairpur

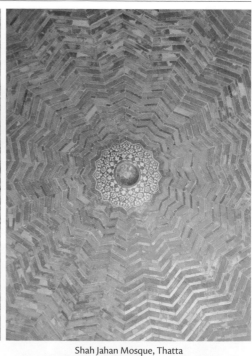

Canopy at Masoom Shah's grave, Sukkur

Shah Jahan Mosque, Thatta

Maryam Zamani Mosque, Lahore

Badshahi Mosque, Lahore

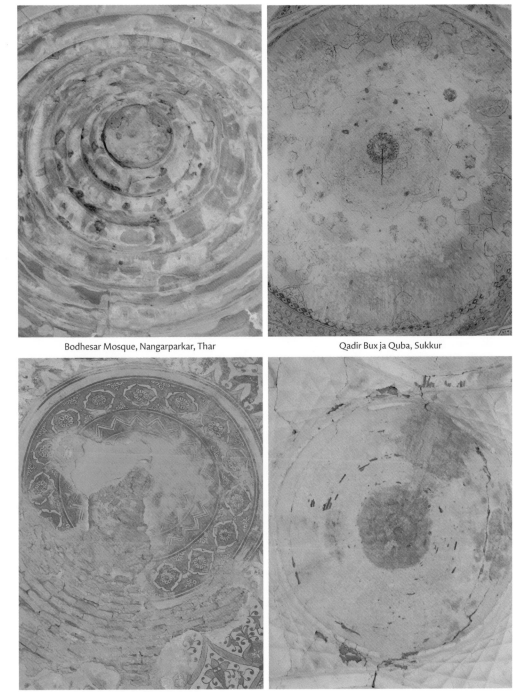

Bodhesar Mosque, Nangarparkar, Thar

Qadir Bux ja Quba, Sukkur

Pat Suleman ja Quba, Dadu

Tomb of Prince Ibrahim, Makli

Gori's Temple, Tharparkar

Gori's temple, Tharparkar

An indigenous hut, Thar

Benazir Park, Karachi

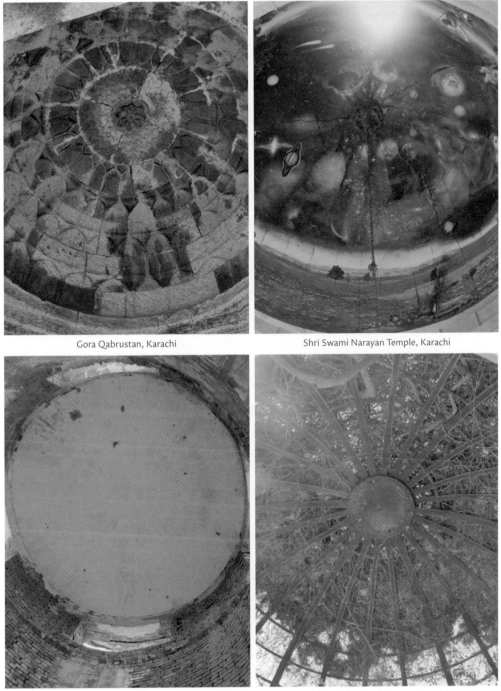

Gora Qabrustan, Karachi

Shri Swami Narayan Temple, Karachi

Derawar Fort, Bahawalpur

Sobhraj Chetumal Terrace, Karachi

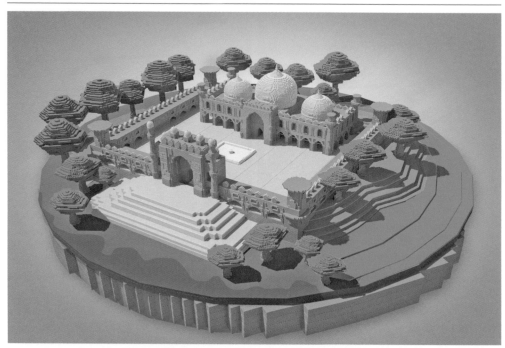

Constructed as a Mosque by Mughal Emperor Aurangzeb (1671–1773)

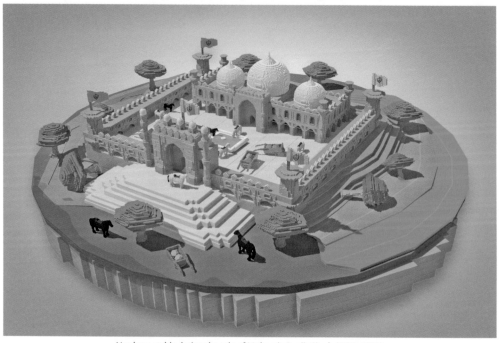

Used as a stable during the rule of Maharaja Ranjit Singh (1799–1839)

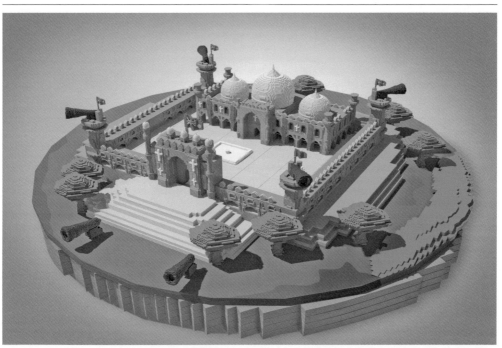

Used as a military garrison during the British Raj (1846–1947)

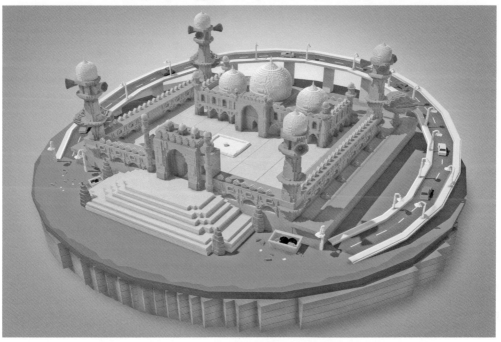

Currently being used as a mosque, major landmark and a tourist attraction (2017)

Naiza Khan

MORIRRO'S FOSSIL

From the eighteenth century onwards, Manora has served as a defense outpost facing the Arabian Sea and forms part of a small archipelago just off the natural harbour of Karachi. Diverse sites of worship continue to mark this terrain on a human scale. They suggest that a multi-religious community once existed on the island. Over the years, however, I have witnessed a particular kind of development, resulting in the slow erasure of both the history and natural ecology of the island. A nexus of military and commercial interests have led to the radical disenfranchisement of Manora's local populations. Manora evokes the metaphor of a body that has been gutted and cast away.

A compelling myth capturing aspects of displacement and belonging was rendered by the great Sindhi poet, Shah Abdul Latif Bhittai (1689–1752). He describes the legend of Morirro and the treacherous sea (also a Sufi analogue of the self and the world). The wise Morirro was handicapped and would stay home when his six brothers would go fishing. When Morirro learnt one day that all six had been swallowed up by a giant shark or a whale, he asked smiths to make him a steel cage (or a glass and steel machine-like structure) with hooks and blades on the outside. Morirro got inside the structure and asked fishermen to tie strong ropes to it and lower it in the treacherous waters between Karachi and Manora. The shark (or whale) swallowed the structure but its blades hooked into the creature's mouth. The fishermen then reeled in the creature and killed it. Morirro safely emerged and cut open the monster's body, finding his brothers' bones. He buried them near Karachi and settled there. These pieces of the "fossil" of Morirro's vessel, a magical and mythical object, have ostensibly been "found" 250 years later. The fragments of this large capsule are washed up on the shore, but imagined here as an amalgam of objects from different time frames. The capsule fragments begin to offer glimpses for imagining other futures that stretch forward indefinitely in the face of larger predatory forces.[1]

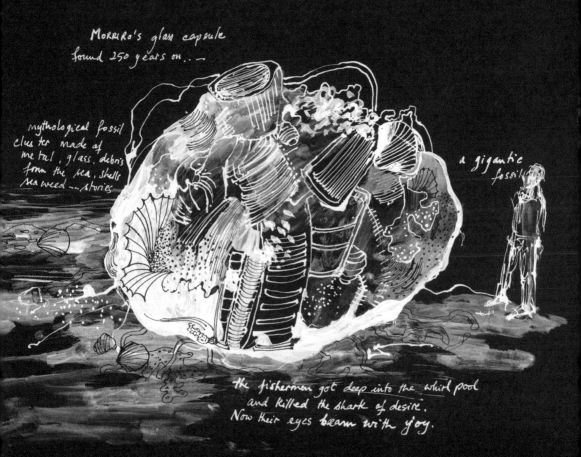

MORIRRO's glass capsule found 250 years on...

mythological fossil cluster made of metal, glass, debris from the sea, shells sea weed... stories.

a gigantic fossil

the fishermen got deep into the whirl pool and killed the shark of desire. Now their eyes beam with joy.

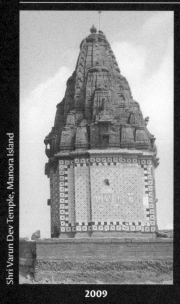  

Shri Varun Dev Temple, Manora Island

2009   **2012**   **2014**

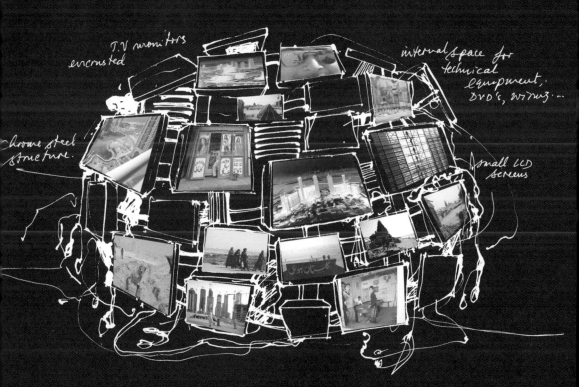

1. Iftikhar Dadi, *Restore the boundaries: The Manora Project*, 2010. pp. 7-8

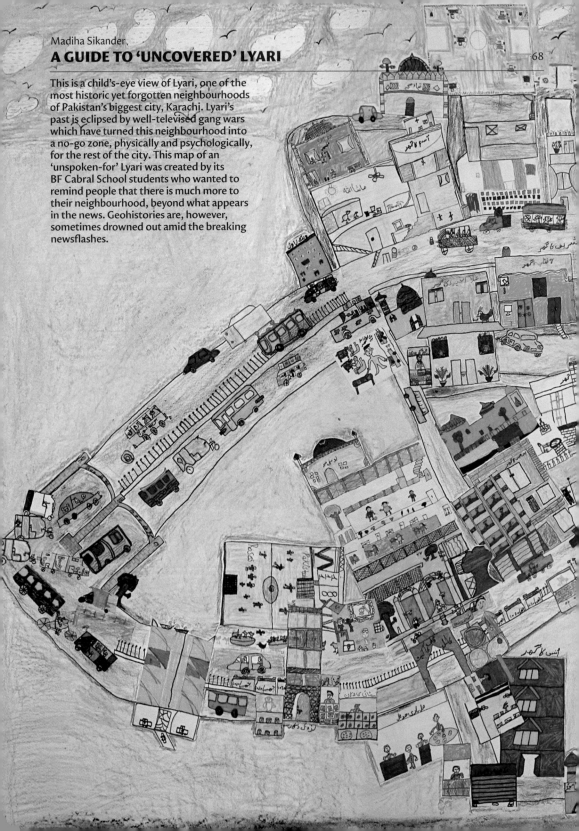

Madiha Sikander,
A GUIDE TO 'UNCOVERED' LYARI

This is a child's-eye view of Lyari, one of the most historic yet forgotten neighbourhoods of Pakistan's biggest city, Karachi. Lyari's past is eclipsed by well-televised gang wars which have turned this neighbourhood into a no-go zone, physically and psychologically, for the rest of the city. This map of an 'unspoken-for' Lyari was created by its BF Cabral School students who wanted to remind people that there is much more to their neighbourhood, beyond what appears in the news. Geohistories are, however, sometimes drowned out amid the breaking newsflashes.

Produced during *Bachon Sey Tabdelee* (Change by Children), a project supported by the Prince Claus Fund

Naila Mahmood

A CITY EMERGES FROM A LABOR ROOM

Sobhraj Chetumal Maternity Hospital is situated in Urdu Bazar, in the heart of downtown Karachi. In a city of more than 22 million inhabitants, Sobhraj is a symbolic epicentre where life converges and emerges—a place where not only human life breathes its first but also where diverse ethnic communities emanate. These babies were born in the same month in a labor room—a place that becomes the mirocosm of the city.

1 Tower, Kharadar
2 Buffer zone, North Karachi
3 Nagan Chowrangi, North Nazimabad
4 Rizvia Colony, Golimar No.2
5 Brigade Police Station, Lines Area
6 Behar Colony, Agra Taj
7 Tonga Stand, Chakiwara
8 Jubliee Market, Bandar Road
9 Gulshan Bahar, Orangi Town
10 Chandni Chowk, Saeedabad, Baldia Town
11 Jafar Tayar Society, Malir
12 Sindhi Hotel, New Karachi
13 Patelpara, Lasbella, Jamshed Town
14 Gujratipara, Soldier Bazar No.1
15 Paka Dhobi Ghaat, Lyari

16 Martin Quarter, Teen Hatti
17 Bakra Piri, Lyari
18 Meena Bazar, PIB Colony
19 Ramzaan Colony, Ranchor Lines
20 Swami Narayan Mandir, Light House
21 Muhajir Camp No.2, Baldia
22 Chel Chowk, Usmanabad
23 Warsia Colony, Orangi Town
24 Jama Majid, Yasinabad
25 Kalakot, Lyari
26 Khajoor Bazar, Lea Market
27 Munzil Pump, Quaidabad, Landhi
28 Iram Bakery, Nazimabad No.2
29 Paracha Chowk, Sher Shah
30 Khokhrapar, Malir
31 Benazir Colony, Hawke's Bay
32 Ghaas Mandi, Ranchor

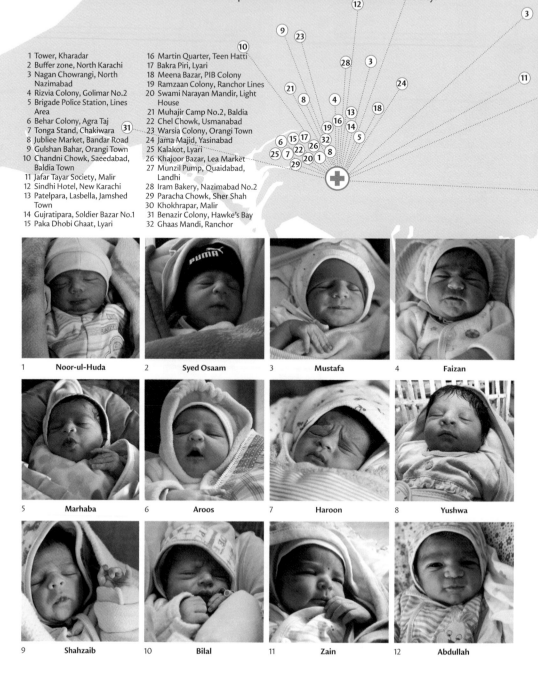

1   Noor-ul-Huda   2   Syed Osaam   3   Mustafa   4   Faizan

5   Marhaba   6   Aroos   7   Haroon   8   Yushwa

9   Shahzaib   10   Bilal   11   Zain   12   Abdullah

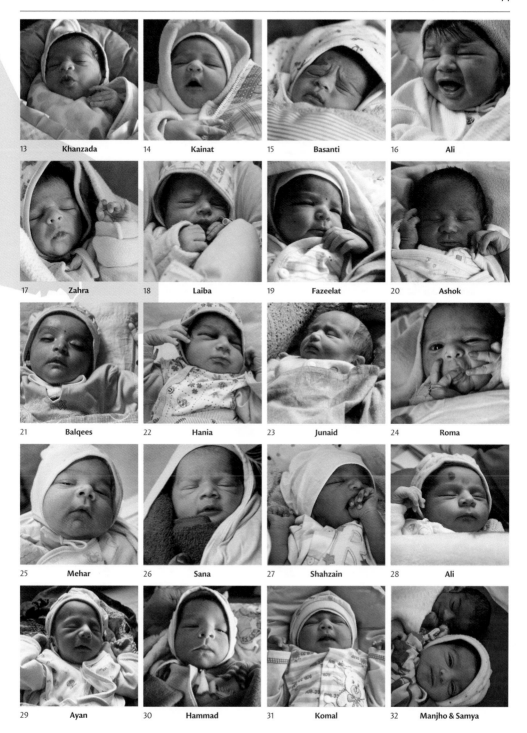

13 Khanzada	14 Kainat	15 Basanti	16 Ali
17 Zahra	18 Laiba	19 Fazeelat	20 Ashok
21 Balqees	22 Hania	23 Junaid	24 Roma
25 Mehar	26 Sana	27 Shahzain	28 Ali
29 Ayan	30 Hammad	31 Komal	32 Manjho & Samya

Headdresses worn by children from the northern to southern regions of Pakistan

Babbu Saab: A rich English gentleman

These images capture the simple act of dressing up for the roles or options prearranged by society. These portrait paintings have been created from my grandfather's photographs to show how he dressed up as an adult in an interpellative act of socialisation. His body became a canvas on which future identities were projected.

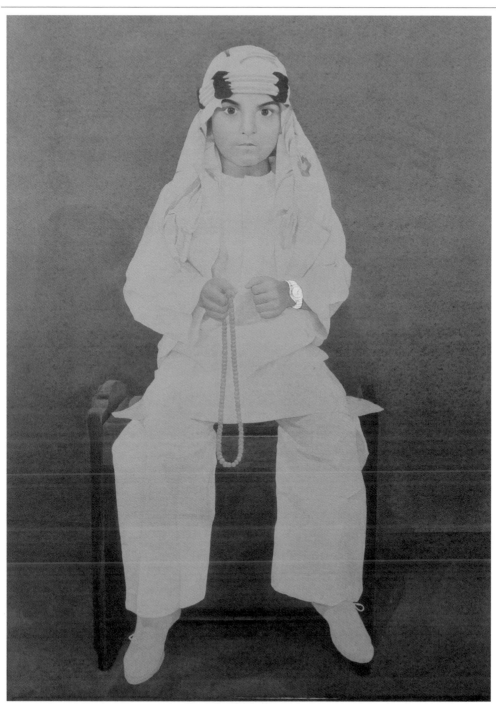

A religious Arab

A helpful scout

A princely groom

These images provide a glimpse into male friendship and brotherhood in Pakistan given the taboo of mixed gender interaction in public spaces. The subjects were photographed by Baba Bhutta of Sheikhupura on a Rooh Kheench camera between 1950 and 1970. Rooh Kheench, translated roughly as spirit- or soul-pulling, acquired its name from the way the photographer would put his hand inside the camera and pull out the photograph.

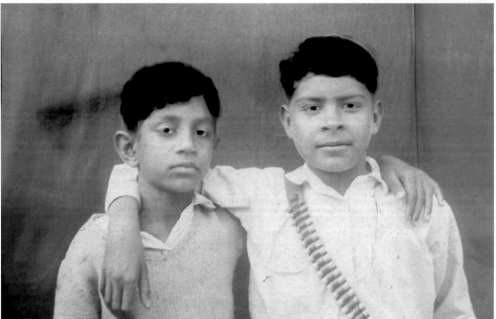

These black and white pictures could thus be taken, printed and sold to the client without the photographer needing a studio or darkroom. This meant that they could set up shop on the pavement near government offices where passport-sized portraits were needed or where tourists could capture a moment in time.

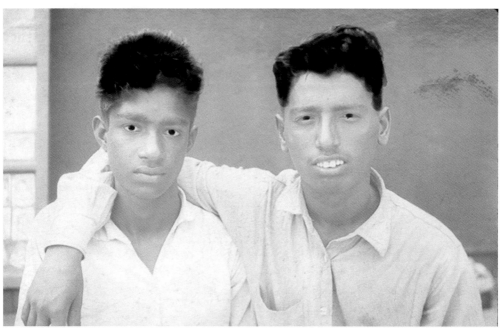

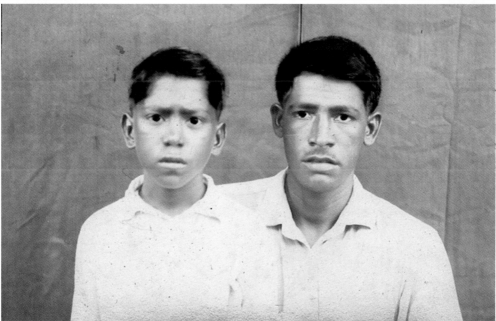

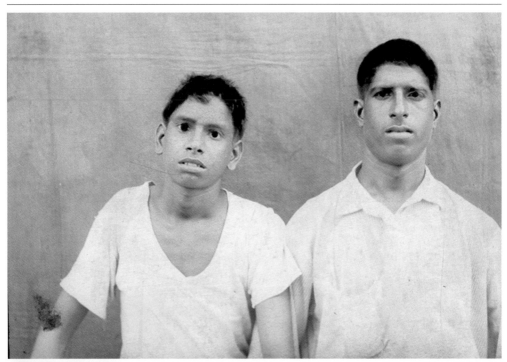

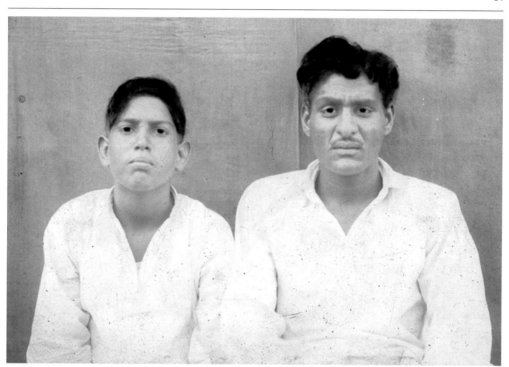

After Partition, many myths and distortions crept into our history books, especially those concerning the father of the nation, Mohammad Ali Jinnah. Ever since his death after the creation of Pakistan, his vision for the country has been constantly reconstructed as state ideology has shifted over the decades. These multiple interpretations of Jinnah's vision have obscured what he really stood for.

Saleh Jaan, Wazir tribe
Wears the yellow *Zyerh Gwali* flower in his cap. This cap, which was originally called the *tepey*,
is now known as the 'dish' thanks to the influx of non-custom paid electronics in the region after the Soviet-Afghan war.
The *Zyerh Gwali*, thankfully, stays the same.

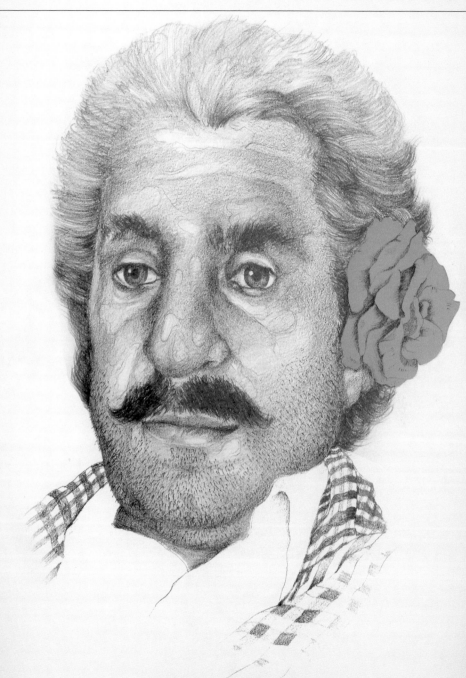

In Pakistan's tribal region Waziristan, the flowers are widely considered a symbol of the 'beloved' as well as that of youth, manliness and inner peace.

Nausher Khan Mehsud, Mehsud tribe
Proud of his moustache and the *Gwalaap* or red rose,
which is grown in every *baethak* or lounging area for men outside a house.

Ashraap Khan, Dawarh tribe
Rebdawan, the bright orange flower is becoming extinct
due to deforestation and ever-increasing population in the region.

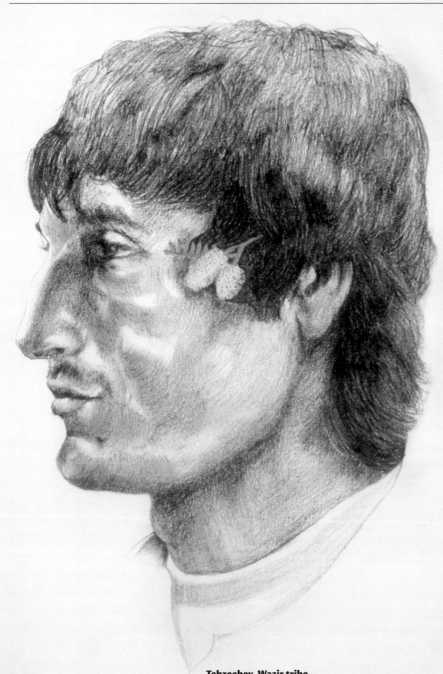

Tehzeebey, Wazir tribe
Found in North Waziristan and Bannu region, the *Paalosa* grows wild,
but people also plant it in their houses as it is both ornamental and fragrant.
This trend is dying, however, as new plants from the outer world are replacing the local ornamental plants.

لائف فگر منیچر پینٹنگ
اسائنمنٹ بانی میڈم طلحہ
سائرہ بی بی
عمل : عثمان سعید نومبر ۱۹۹۷ء

میرا نام سائرہ بی بی ہے۔۱۶ سال کی عمر میں شادی ہوئی۔ میرے ۶ بچے ہیں۔ ۲ بچے اور ۴ بچیاں ہیں۔
میاں راج مزدوری کرتا ہے۔ حمید بابا میرے محلے دار ہیں۔ ۶ سال پہلے نیشنل کالج لے کر آنے یہاں دیہاڑی کے
حساب سے ۶ گھنٹے کی کلاس میں ماڈلنگ کے ۱۲۰ روپے اور ۴ گھنٹے کے ۸۰ روپے ملتے ہیں۔ تھک بہت جاتی ہوں۔

My name is Saira Bibi. I got married at the age of 16. I have two sons and four daughters. My husband works as a labourer. Hameed Baba lives in my street and 6 years ago he brought me to National College of Arts. Everyday I get Rs. 120 for modelling for 6 hours and Rs. 80 for 4 hours. I get really tired after the day's job.

89

ماسٹر ریاض

لاہور مئی ۲۰۱۵ء

عمل: عثمان سعید

میرا نام ریاض ہے۔ عمر آٹھ سال ہے۔ جب پانچ سال کا تھا، ماں باپ حادثے میں چل بسے۔ بڑا بھائی ہے اور تین چھوٹی بہنیں ہیں۔ حادثے سے اب تک بھائی کے ساتھ موٹر ورکشاپ میں کام کر رہا ہوں۔ یہاں دیہاڑی کے حساب سے ایک دن کے ۱۰۰ سے ۲۰۰ روپے تک ملتے ہیں۔ تھک بہت جاتا ہوں۔ سکول جانے اور پڑھنے کو دل کرتا ہے۔

My name is Riaz. The age is eight. When I was five, my parents passed away in an accident. Got an elder brother and three younger sisters. Been working at a mechanic's workshop with my brother since the accident. By the daily wage, I can earn between one hundred to two hundred rupees. I get quite exhausted. I really feel like going to school and studying.

These are the covers of leading digests, tabloid and fashion magazines published in one month. Women digests and tabloids are published as monthly magazines that contain melodramatic narratives of feminine domesticity, love and victimization primarily

written by and for women and sometimes, written by men as women. The exaggeration in stories creates fantasized storylines or pictorial content consumed mostly by young women and, in case of suspense and mystery digests, by older men as well.

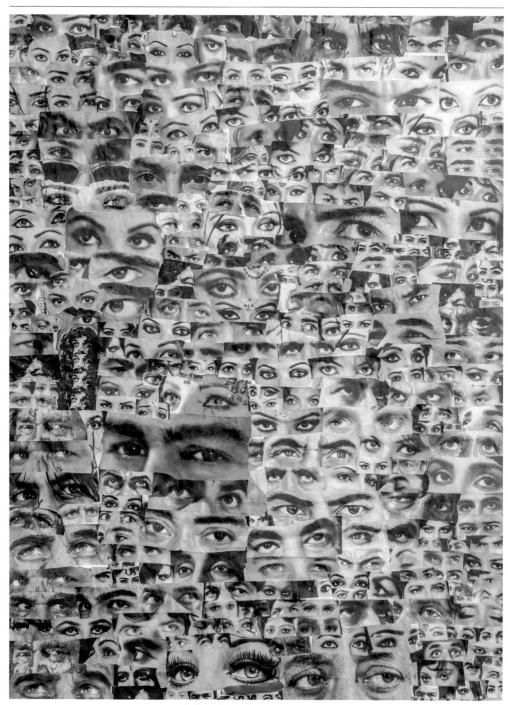

Heroes and villians from Pakistani film posters, 1975–2015

Censored skins from Pakistani film posters, 1975–2015

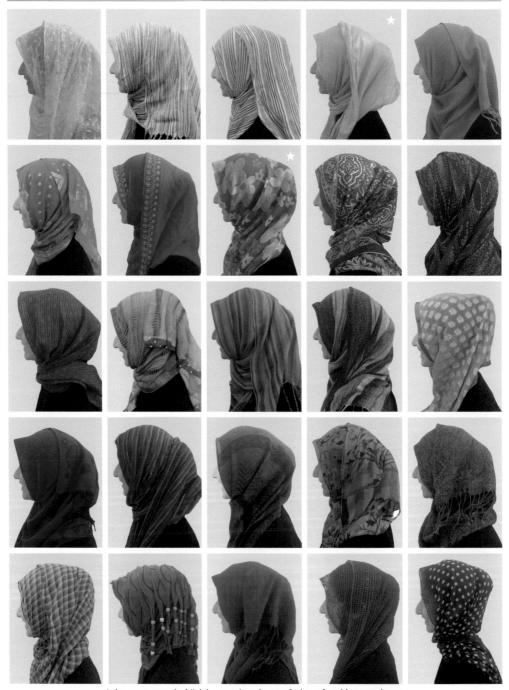

I choose to wear the hijab because it makes me feel comfortable around men.
Since it has become a part of my everyday clothing, I now have a pretty large collection.

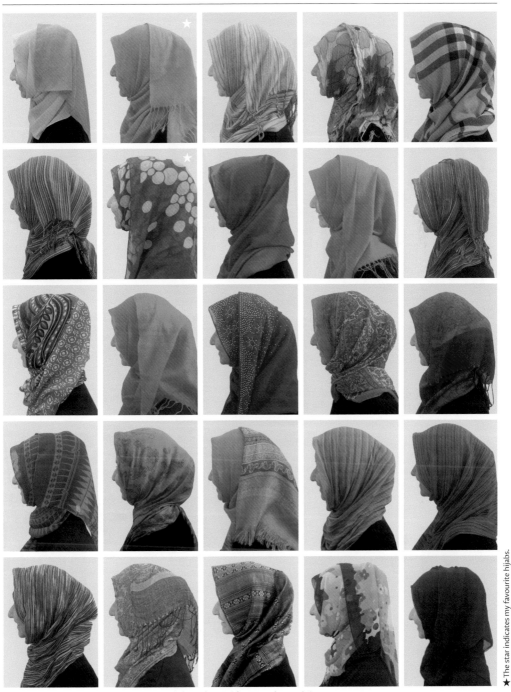

★ The star indicates my favourite hijabs.

I share them with my mother and sister.
We wear them to work, to school, the market and to parties.

January
Eid Milad-un-Nabi
(12th Rabi-ul-Awal)

February
On the screening of Pakistan versus
India cricket Match

March
On the night before final
presentation of the Subjective Atlas

April
On sister's wedding

May
During summer football camp
as a goalkeeper

June
At Bohra friend's milad ceremony

July
On Eid prayers at Eid-ul-Fitr
(1st Shawal)

August
On the Independence Day
(14th August)

September
During my trip to Naran,
Northern Areas

October
On Eid-ul-Adha 'Festival of the
Sacrifice' as a butcher
(10th Zil-Hajj)

November
On Youm-e-Ashour
(10th Muharram)

December
During semester holidays
at home

Almost everyday
Artist at university

Soon
During my job hunting days after
graduation to secure a decent job

After
On my 'maiyon' (a pre-wedding
ceremony), hopefully after finding a
beautiful wife

Finally
On my wedding day
as a groom!

THE NEW SUIT

For an average Pakistani woman, buying and making a new suit for every occasion is not a matter of luxury, it is a necessity. If one wants to explore the aesthetics of a common female in Pakistan, a cloth market is the best place to go to.

Alina (25) **'For a Muharram majlis'**

Shehnaz (40) **'For a Christmas party'**

Tahera (44) **'As winter wear for the evenings'**

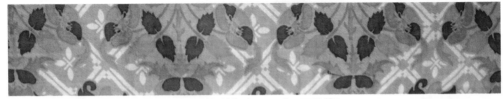

Hajra (25) **'For brother's dholki'**

Afsa (28) **'For kid's parent-teacher meeting'**

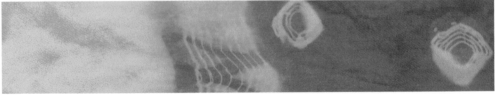

Ambreen (36) **'As a semi-formal dress for the office'**

The material ranges from expensive designer couture to floral prints bought from the Khan bhai selling clothes on the footpath. This new suit is the statement that identifies individuals at every event under the sun marked in the calendar.

Alyza (34) **'For Eid Milad un Nabi (PBUH)'**

Javeria (19) **'For first day of university'**

Shiza (22) **'For New Year's Eve'**

Maham (22) **'For a cousin's wedding'**

Nighat (52) **'As a gift for daughter's Godh Bharai'**

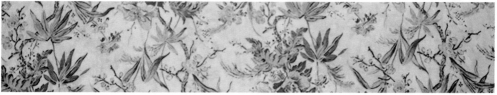

Sobia (17) **'As a gift for Nani'**

Inheritance or collection of real or artificial jewellery is one of the older traditions in most families. It is believed that the bride is never complete without dazzling jewellery sets, and as a result family is seen as being even richer, which is one of the main motivations for collecting it in a majority of households.

Sassi's Seraiki jewellery
Self bought, artificial, popular with working class, collecting since 2006.
A ring with a red stone was passed on to her by her paternal grandmother and has been in the family since the 1950s
Estimated value of the ring: Rs. 32,000 | Average monthly household income: Rs. 15,000 | Estimated value of the collection: Rs. 600

Mariam's Punjabi jewellery
Inherited as dowry, pure gold, collecting since 2003.
Average monthly household income: Rs. 40,000 | Estimated value: Rs. 500,000

Besides being a reflection of taste, status and culture, for some, jewellery also acts as a safe investment that can be sold in case of a dire emergency.

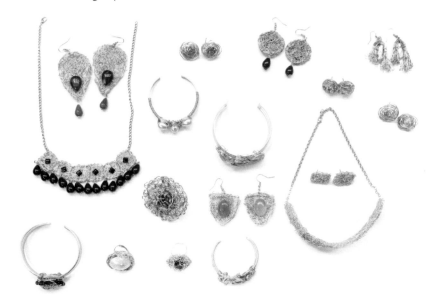

Afshan's artificial jewellery
Self bought, collecting since 2010.
Estimated value of earrings: Rs. 1,200 | Estimated value of the collection: Rs. 27,000

Afshan's local jewellery
Inherited, pure gold. Her family had been collecting it for her wedding since 1984.
Monthly household income: Rs. 95,000 | Estimated value of the collection: Rs. 400,000

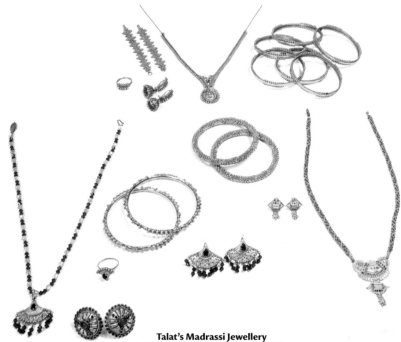

Talat's Madrassi Jewellery
Self bought, pure gold, collecting since 2013.
Monthly household income: Rs. 45,000 | Estimated value: Rs. 350,000

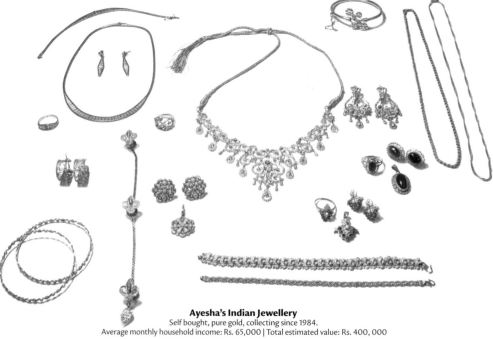

Ayesha's Indian Jewellery
Self bought, pure gold, collecting since 1984.
Average monthly household income: Rs. 65,000 | Total estimated value: Rs. 400, 000

Sarah's Indian jewellery
Inherited from her family, collecting since 1920s. The green set belonged to her great grand aunt and has been passed down generations.

Sarah's Hyderabadi jewellery
Inherited, pure gold. Her family had been collecting it for her wedding since 1984.
Monthly household income: Rs. 95,000 | Estimated value of the collection: Rs. 400,000

The neologism 'lotacracy' was coined in Pakistan to describe politicians whose loyalties are constantly shifting as they switch parties. The term originates from an old school spherical lota without a base, which tended to roll over in unpredictable directions when kept on uneven ground.

The modern-day version of the lota is the plastic watering can: inexpensive, lightweight, and widely available. However, in most public and domestic washrooms in the urban centres, the lota has been replaced by 'Muslim' showers. Yet the lota is considered mandatory in private and public washrooms across the country.

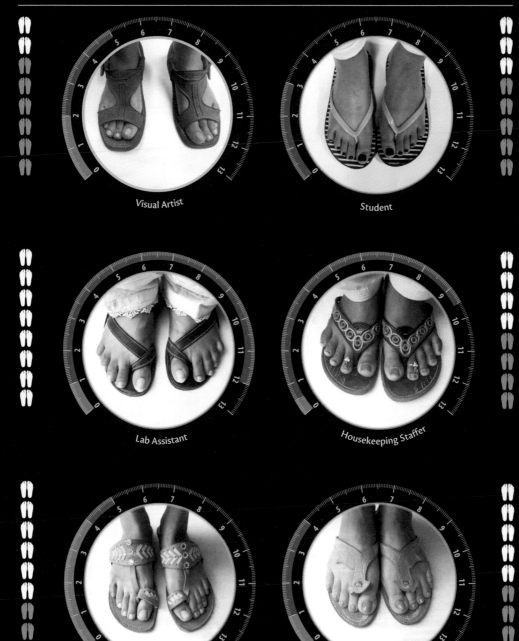

Visual Artist

Student

Lab Assistant

Housekeeping Staffer

Student

Senior Executive

Number of times feet washed in a day

Hours walked out of need

Hours walked out of own will

Prompted by a mild foot fetish, I began my 24-Feet Journey with casual observations of people's feet (and their shoes) at my work place.

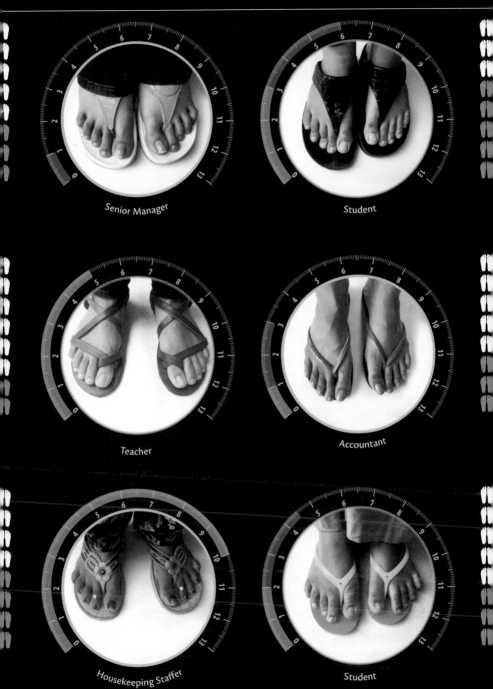

Senior Manager

Student

Teacher

Accountant

Housekeeping Staffer

Student

This pedometer matrix reinforced a counter-intuitive perception around feet usage, their daily exertion, hygiene,

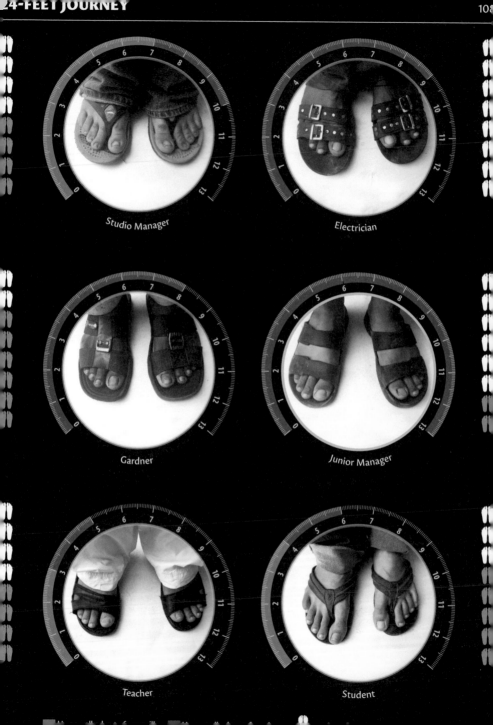

Studio Manager

Electrician

Gardner

Junior Manager

Teacher

Student

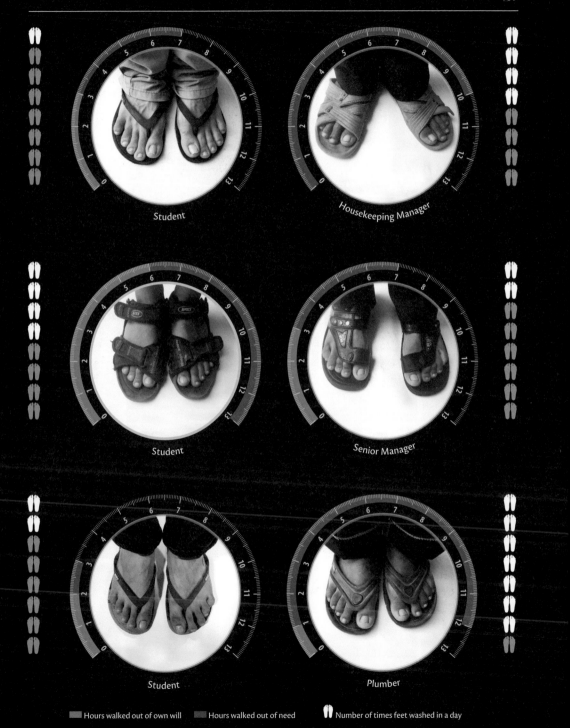

Student

Housekeeping Manager

Student

Senior Manager

Student

Plumber

Hours walked out of own will　　Hours walked out of need　　Number of times feet washed in a day

As with any other big city, millions of inhabitants of Karachi come out every morning to start a new day. For the past three years, I have been seeing these people from different professions on the verge of crossing the road on their way to work every morning.

For me, these people stand there with anticipation and expectations, ready to embark upon their respective journeys, not unlike myself.

Driving on Karachi's roads is an adventure because of how fellow commuters arbitrarily interpret road safety and rules. Indeed many drivers depart from the demarcated lanes to make up their own as they go along. My experience travelling on one of the busiest roads in Karachi is mapped here to show my encounters with motorized and non-motorized transport and how they affect my journey.

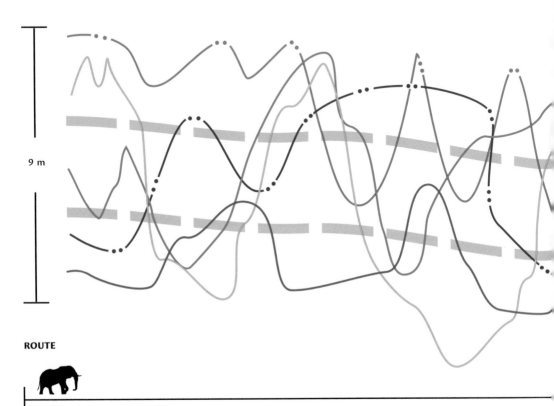

9 m

ROUTE

Safari Park 9.9 km

CAPACITY

- ■ Seating capacity (black)
- ■ Crush capacity (grey)
- ■ Adults
- ● Children

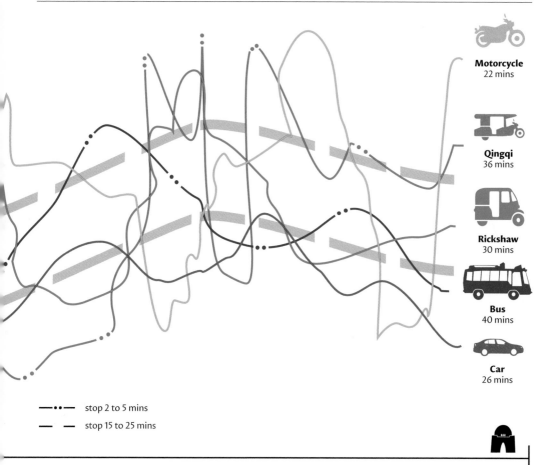

Motorcycle
22 mins

Qingqi
36 mins

Rickshaw
30 mins

Bus
40 mins

Car
26 mins

—••— stop 2 to 5 mins

— — stop 15 to 25 mins

Mazaar-e-Quaid

HURDLES

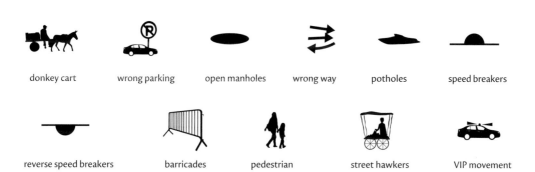

donkey cart   wrong parking   open manholes   wrong way   potholes   speed breakers

reverse speed breakers   barricades   pedestrian   street hawkers   VIP movement

Since its inception in 1729, Karachi was always a cosmopolitan city of Hindus and Muslims, along with Jews, Parsis, Iranians, and Goans. Together they administered the city with great harmony. With Partition and the cross exodus of Hindus and Muslims, then the declaration of Pakistan as an Islamic republic in 1977, followed by a military-cum-Islamic dictatorship, the country acquired a monolithic Islamic identity. Many prominent streets and roads were renamed to commemorate national personalities or evoke a romanticized Muslim heritage or in some cases to de-commemorate, e.g. Motilal Nehru Road (the father of India's post-Partition leader, Nehru) which was renamed Jigar Muradabadi Road after a national poet. Walking through the streets of the old city, it comes as a surprise to see how many of the old names survive, Hindu, Parsi, Christian even a few Jewish names. Is it because these areas are 'below the political radar'? Does it indicate an acceptance and assimilation of the city's true history?

- BRITISH
- CHRISTIAN
- HINDU
- JEWISH
- MUSLIM
- PARSI

ABIGAIL STREET **AKBAR ROAD** ADVANI STREET BARNES STREET **KHURIA STREET** BLENKEN STREET **SARMAN ROAD** ELLIS STREET RAGHOO STREET **MIRAN PIR STREET MIR MOHAMMAD BALOCH STREET** MAJOR BUCKLAND ROAD **CHAPEL STREET** RAMPART ROW NEWNHAM ROAD **D KHOJA QABRISTAN STREET ST PATRICK STREET** SHIVDAS STREET EMPRESS STREET **BANTWA GALI JUMA BALOCH ROAD** SHIVSHAN CHHIPA STREET BOMBAY STREET DOSABHAI GHADYALI STREET CARRY ROAD A. F. FERGUSON STREET **NAZIR HUSSAIN ROAD** RAM TALAO ROAD **BHURGARI ROAD** WILLIAM STREET **BEGUM SAHIBA NAVAJBAI STREET** RANCHORE ROAD ELLENBOROUGH STREET WALLACE ROAD **DAIS STREET NOOMAN ROAD** GRANT ROAD GENERAL RICHARDSON ROAD SHIV RATAN STREET **IQBAL SHAHEED ROAD** KISHAN CHAND CHELARAM ROAD **TAIMANI STREET UMAR LANE ZOHRA STREET** OUTRAM ROAD CLAYTON ROAD NARISH CHANDRA STREET GEORGE STREET MCHINCH ROAD KHOONSHAL RAI LANE ROSE LANE ABRAHAM STREET GLOUCESTER STREET **IMAM BARGHA STREET** GRIEG STREET **ZIKRI PARA ROAD** IRELAND ROAD RUTTAN STREET **D'ABRO ROAD** SAVANTI ROAD GERMAN STREET H. J. BEHRANA PARSI DAR-E-MEHER ASHOKA STREET SHELDON ROAD SHIVRAM DEWAN MAL ROAD DIYARAM GHIDUMAL ROAD **ESFANDIYAR STREET** STRACHAN ROAD TABOOT LANE KENYA STREET LONDON DERRY STREET DENSO ROAD MOMBASA STREET DIYARAM STREET DALAL STREET HIRANAND STREET **MAJID ROAD** RÃMCHANDRA TEMPLE ROAD CASTLE STREET SEETAL DAS STREET **NAZARETH ROAD** SAVANTI ROAD AJMER STREET **SEQUIRES STREET** COLOMBO STREET AJA MAWJI STREET ALI BUDHA STREET SILVER STREET ABDEALI SAIFUDDIN STREET DADABHOY NAUROJI ROAD TAHER SAIFUDDIN STREET BOHRI ROAD HAJI ABDUL SHAKOOR STREET KASBAAN STREET SHAHBAZ STREET ROAD DADABHOY NAUROJI ROAD MOSES IBN EZRA STREET UDHAM DAS TARA CHAND ROAD EDWARD STREET RAJKOT STREET MILL STREET CONNOR STREET HARI CHAND RAI ROAD **SHAH ABDUL LATIF ROAD** MUSKET ROAD VIOLET STREET MAGAIN SHALOME SYNAGOGUE VISHRAMDAS SUKHRAMDAS STREET TRADEY STREET **NOOR MASJID STREET** SLOANE STREET **MIR SHER MOHAMMAD ROAD** JEHANGIR PUNTHAKEY ROAD FAKIR M. DURA KHAN ROAD MONGTOMERY STREET PILGRIM ROAD **D'MELLO ROAD** KUFA STREET **ST MARY STREET** JAGOO MAI BHAGOO MAL STREET SOLOMON DAVID ROAD **MAHMUD SHAH ROAD** PARR STREET **MASJID-E-TAYYABA STREET** MITHIBAI STREET **GABOL ROAD** MCLEAN STREET RUSTAMJI STREET SHEROK LINE SARDAR STREET PENOLO ROAD GHOSIA GALI PANJRAPUR STREET **ZAINABIA ROAD PEDRO D'SOUZA ROAD** RIZVI SHAHEED ROAD TAGORE STREET **MIR AYUB KHAN ROAD** KEMBALL ROAD ADAM UMAR STREET UDHAY RAM STREET NAUROJI CRESCENT PRESTONJI STREET BELFAST STREET TAPP STREET SACCHAL FAQIR ROAD MURAD KHAN ROAD LOTUS STREET **BADSHAH ROAD** PARSU RAM DESH ROAD JACOB LINE HUMER ROAD JHAMRAI STREET MARSHAL STREET **HAJI CHANDU STREET** GAWALI LANE MUKHI CHAITRAM ROAD **MEMON STREET** MARKWICK ROAD WEDDERBURN ROAD **MISQUITE ROAD** JEEVAN STREET **IQBAL MARKET ROAD** PRICE ROAD

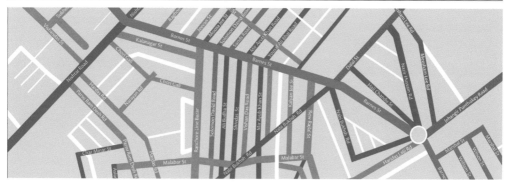

Ranchore Line Area, Old City

JUTLAND STREET YOUSUF STREET **D'SILVA STREET** SCANDAL POINT ROAD GULBAI STREET BRITTO ROAD FAQIR M. DURA KHAN SABRIA STREET TIRATH DAS ROAD TAGRUR STREET TAUFIQUE STREET WELLINGTON STREET MOHAN ROAD REHMAT AVENUE JAM STREET DEPOT LINES SOLDIER BAZAAR ROAD JUMA GALI RAMJI SOMAYA ROAD **LOBO STREET** DIN MOHAMMAD WAFAI ROAD **FATHER GIMINEZ STREET** COMMISSARIAT ROAD MALABAR STREET **BAWA ROAD** VERLEY ROAD YASIR SHORT WAY MIRZA STREET TALPUR STREET SOHRAB KATRAK ROAD SAIFY STREET ZARINA BALOCH STREET JAI RAM STREET ROAD MARSTON ROAD MALAY STREET LAKSHMAN STREET DEVI STREET HINGORABAD ROAD SALEH MUHAMMAD PANJGURI ROAD BHICAJI STREET RUSTAMJI STREET KHANJI TULSIDAS STREET NOORANI HASSAN ALI EFFENDI ROAD JAMSHED MEHTA ROAD KHOJA STREET NARAYAN TEMKER ROAD ABU MANZIL GALI JAGDAL STREET MOOSA LANE KARIM BHAI KARANJI STREET WEBB STREET SHEEDI VILLAGE ROAD TEHRAN ROAD BABAR SHAH STREET HANUMAN STREET JHULE LAL STREET SADHU HIRANAND STREET MANEOKJI STREET MEREWETHER ROAD SHAHANI STREET DR SYEDNA MOHAMMAD BURHANUD-DIN ROAD BAGH-E-ZEHRA STREET BOHRAPIR STREET SOBRAJ CHATTU MAL STREET KOTWAL STREET HIRA RAM STREET IQBAL HOTI ROAD RAM SAMAI STREET HART DAVIES ROAD NATMAN STREET LOVE LANE GRACE STREET **ADAMJEE BUDHA BHAI STREET** PRATT ROAD MAKGI BHAWANI ROAD ASHKENAZI STREET ARMENIAN STREET MEGHJI BHANG-WANI ROAD **MUHAMMAD ALI ALVI ROAD** PRINCE AVENUE DURRANI STREET SOPARIVA-LA STREET ZAYDI LANE BALMIKI STREET KAZI KHUDA BAKSH ROAD JAGNATH STREET H. J. BEHRANA PARSI DAR-E-MEHER JHANSI STREET OLIVE STREET RAMJI STREET NABIDAD LANE MUHAMMAD HASHIM GAZDAR ROAD NABI BUX ROAD NAJAF STREET SUKHRAMDAS STREET AFSHANI STREET JESWANI STREET BARGHA HUSSAINI STREET **ST JOSEPH STREET CHURCH STREET** RAM BHARTI STREET ASLAM ROAD JAIN STREET VISHAN DAS ROAD NAPIER ROAD EMBANKMENT ROAD **D'CRUZ ROAD** JAMES TERRACE SHAMBU NATH STREET PRINCE STREET **NUSSERWANJI ROAD** MORE STREET PARK LANE HARI CHAND RAI ROAD **HAJI PIR MOHAMMAD ROAD** BEMBRIDGE ROAD ASHOKA STREET WILSON STREET **HASSAN ALI STREET** ZANZIBAR STREET AGA KHAN STREET CHAGATAI ROAD HUS-SAIN SHAH SHAHEED ROAD FRERE ROAD **MAMA PARSI ROAD** NATHIN AMARA ROAD ALFRED STREET ORANGE STREET LALA JASWANT RAI ROAD HOSKING ROAD OJHA ROAD B. ADVANI ROAD **BAHADUR SHAH STREET** MASJID ROAD BEDIAN ROAD SCOTLAND STREET **FRAMROSE ROAD** ROBSON ROAD PITEMBER STREET PEARL STREET REW RAJLAL STREET GOLD STREET CHANDAN MUKHI LANE REXER LANE **DR BILMORIA ROAD** VINE STREET FLYNN STREET RAMDAS STREET SANDS ROAD KHARE GHAT ROAD **MIRZA ADAM KHAN ROAD** VINCENT STREET **SINGO LANE GEHRAM KHAN STREET** HARDAS STREET BELLASIS STREET **MOJAHED STREET** BEAUMONT ROAD ASSUMAL BAWAPAT STREET ELANDER ROAD NICHOLAS STREET NARAYAN STREET MESHAM LEA ROAD **DR PIRES ROAD JOSEPH D'AMNO ROAD** MANSFIELD STREET KALYAN JEE STREET DUNDAS STREET

Landhi Town, Karachi

My home

Police Station

No street lights

Non-functional street lights

The route I use to go home at night

The route I use to go home during the day

34 points of unreported mugging cases during
the last five months because of no street lights

2 points where I have been mugged during
the last five months because of no street lights

Sana Abrar (22) mugged twice
Carries Nokia X1 & Samsung Galaxy

Daniya Pervez (43) mugged once
Carries Nokia 105 & iPhone 5

Ayesha Fatima (20) mugged once
Carries HTC Desire & Samsung S2

Asad Salam (21) mugged 4 times
Carries Nokia 1600 & iPhone 5

Qunitah Bukhari (22) mugged once
Carris Nokia 110 &Samsung S4 Mini

Abbas Ali (42) mugged 4 times
Carries Nokia105 & iPhone 6 Plus

Saad Khan (38) mugged thrice
Carries Q Mobile Q5 & LG Optimus

Samina Rohail (50) mugged once
Carries Touchtel Craze & Nokia Lumia

Sana Zarar (21) never been mugged
Carries Motorola W230 & Nokia Lumia

According to the two-phone theory of Karachi, to avoid any major loss in the event of mugging, one must try to carry two phones; a cheaper decoy one for the robber and a better one for oneself.

Arsalan Haneef, Graphic Designer
Carries Rs 300, 2 debit, 1 mastercard,
motorcycle document and CNIC copy
Robbed twice, prefers plastic money now

Asim Ali Khan, Editor of a Newspaper
Carries Rs 200, 1 debit, 1 mastercard,
car document copy and press card
Never been robbed but carries plastic money

Rahil Ahmad Khan, Teacher
Carries Rs 250, some business cards
and only a few documents
Never been robbed but stays careful

Shehzad Khan, Male Model
Carries Rs 500, photos of his father and late brother,
CNIC copy, business cards and some documents
Never been robbed

Nazim Khan, Electrician
Carries Rs 4,750, Motorcycle document,
CNIC copy and some business cards
Robbed seven times but not afraid any more

Hafiz Muhammad Farhan, Journalist
Carries Rs 950, motorbike document
and press card
Never been robbed

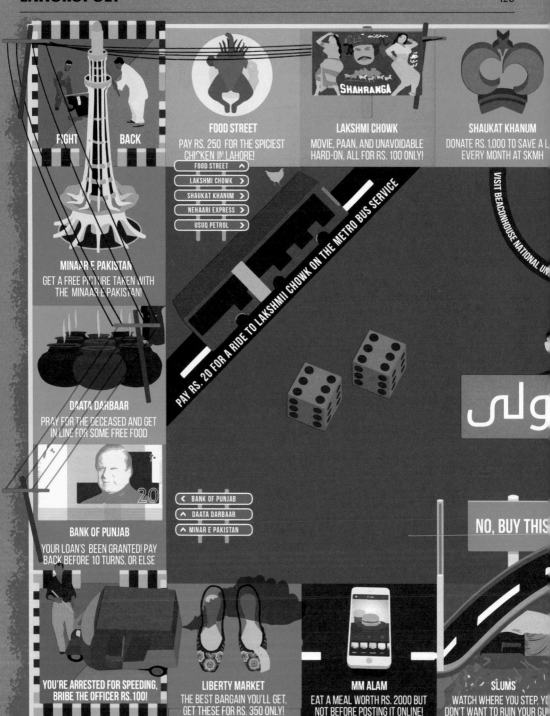

FOOD STREET
PAY RS. 250 FOR THE SPICIEST
CHICKEN IN LAHORE!

- FOOD STREET
- LAKSHMI CHOWK
- SHAUKAT KHANUM
- NEHAARI EXPRESS
- USUQ PETROL

LAKSHMI CHOWK
MOVIE, PAAN, AND UNAVOIDABLE
HARD-ON, ALL FOR RS. 100 ONLY!

SHAHRANGA

SHAUKAT KHANUM
DONATE RS. 1,000 TO SAVE A L
EVERY MONTH AT SKMH

FIGHT   BACK

MINAAR E PAKISTAN
GET A FREE PICTURE TAKEN WITH
THE MINAAR E PAKISTAN!

VISIT BEACONHOUSE NATIONAL UN

PAY RS. 20 FOR A RIDE TO LAKSHMII CHOWK ON THE METRO BUS SERVICE

DAATA DARBAAR
PRAY FOR THE DECEASED AND GET
IN LINE FOR SOME FREE FOOD

20

BANK OF PUNJAB
YOUR LOAN'S BEEN GRANTED! PAY
BACK BEFORE 10 TURNS, OR ELSE

- BANK OF PUNJAB
- DAATA DARBAAR
- MINAR E PAKISTAN

NO, BUY THIS

**YOU'RE ARRESTED FOR SPEEDING,
BRIBE THE OFFICER RS. 100!**

LIBERTY MARKET
THE BEST BARGAIN YOU'LL GET,
GET THESE FOR RS. 350 ONLY!

MM ALAM
EAT A MEAL WORTH RS. 2000 BUT
NOT BEFORE POSTING IT ONLINE!

SLUMS
WATCH WHERE YOU STEP, YO
DON'T WANT TO RUIN YOUR GU

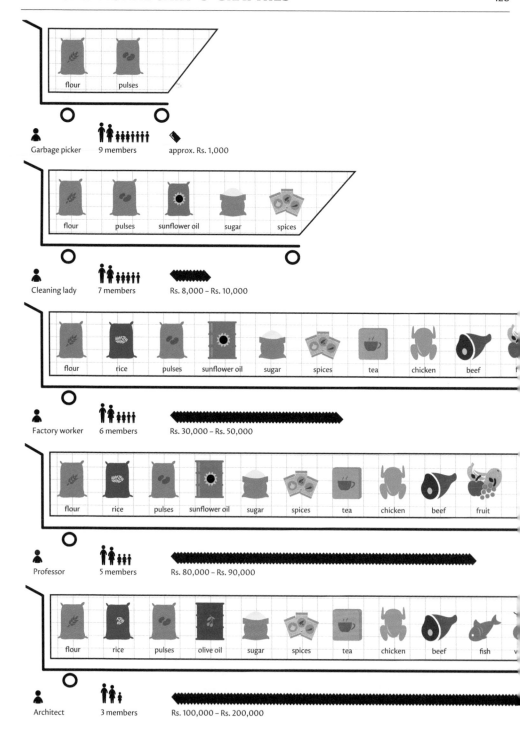

Garbage picker | 9 members | approx. Rs. 1,000
flour · pulses

Cleaning lady | 7 members | Rs. 8,000 – Rs. 10,000
flour · pulses · sunflower oil · sugar · spices

Factory worker | 6 members | Rs. 30,000 – Rs. 50,000
flour · rice · pulses · sunflower oil · sugar · spices · tea · chicken · beef · f

Professor | 5 members | Rs. 80,000 – Rs. 90,000
flour · rice · pulses · sunflower oil · sugar · spices · tea · chicken · beef · fruit

Architect | 3 members | Rs. 100,000 – Rs. 200,000
flour · rice · pulses · olive oil · sugar · spices · tea · chicken · beef · fish · v

These are recordings from the grocery lists of five families belonging to different income groups. They show their purchasing power at the start of each month. The size of the family is inversely proportionate to the amount of food they can afford.

 profession

monthly income in 1000 rupees

family members

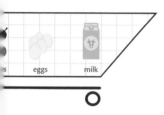

	eggs	milk

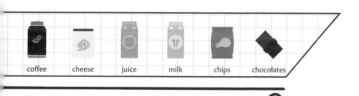

coffee	cheese	juice	milk	chips	chocolates

eggs	honey	coffee	cheese	juice	milk	soft drinks	chips	cookies	chocolates

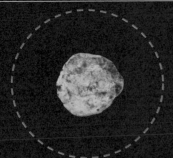

Inara (3)
I want to make roti like my mum

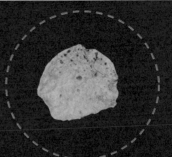

Raheen (5)
Just for fun

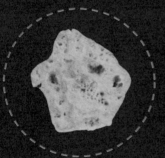

Anabiya (7)
I love cooking

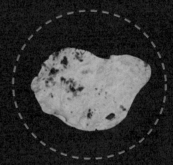

Mazna (9)
I want to join Masterchef Junior

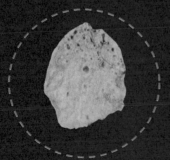

Afhsan (11)
To make my Daddy happy

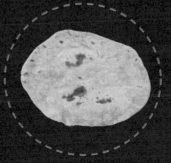

Mahwish (13)
Because my cousin makes it

All the success of the world lies on one side, and the skill to cook the perfect roti on another.
Women are judged for all sorts of attributes: their looks, manners and abilities.

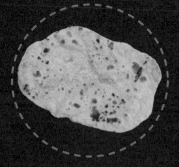

Amal (15)
To protect myself from Daadi's wrath

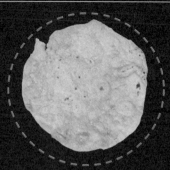

Eeshaa (18)
To upload pictures on Instagram

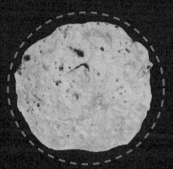

Soha (20)
Preparing myself for married life

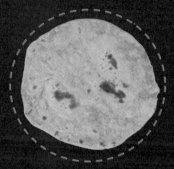

Nida (23)
To show I can manage work as well as the house chores

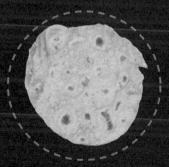

Maria (25)
To impress my in-laws and husband

Zohra (39)
For my family

In Pakistan, making a perfectly round 'roti' (or 'chapati') is the hallmark of the perfect 'marriageable girl'. Round or not, they are rotis and no matter what the shape, should be given the respect the effort deserves.

In Pakistan, like the rest of South Asian countries, tea is the most popular beverage and holds an integral significance in local culture. Since South Asia was part of the British Commonwealth for many years and as a result of that connection a considerable volume of the local population and their life styles have been influenced by the British style and etiquette of drinking tea, which is formal and somewhat conservative. In a postcolonial Pakistani society, however, a dhaba or roadside stall tea drinking culture has evolved its own style and etiquette which is, in a way, the complete juxtaposition of the British style.*

CASUALLY EXCHANGE
DIVERSE CONVERSATIONS

*Dhaba is the name given to roadside restaurants in Pakistan. They are located on highways and generally serve local cuisine, and also serve as truck stops. They are most commonly found next to petrol stations, and are open 24 hours a day.

COW'S MILK

IS A **MUST ADD**
IN A *BREWED or*
NON-BREWED TEA

DIP or DUNK
ONE'S BISCUIT
OR
*PARATHA
INTO THE TEA CUP

UNDER
NO CONDITIONS
WOULD THESE BE
CONSIDERED
PRIMITIVE

YOU MAY
GAZE OVER
THE TEA CUP
OFTEN YOUR EYES
MAY MEET WITH
ANOTHER

SIP
OR
SLURP

YOUR
TEA
FROM A CUP
OR
SAUCER

**THIS TYPE OF
BEHAVIOUR IS NOT
CONSIDERED IMPROPER**

HOLD
THE TEA CUP
SATISFYINGLY

WITH **THE THUMB
AND FINGER**
or
**GRASP THE BOTTOM
OF THE CUP
IN YOUR HAND**

DON'T FEEL SHY
ASKING FOR

MORE
TEA!

* A paratha is a flatbread and is an important part of a traditional South Asian breakfast. Traditionally, it is made using ghee but oil is also used. Paratha is an amalgamation of the words parat and atta which literally means layers of cooked dough.

An estimated 87% of homes in Karachi own television sets. They have always been seen as much more than just an appliance; they are a status symbol, a coveted dowry item that commands respect upon acquisition. They are also valued as a source of

entertainment—a window to the world in a place where not everyone can afford a computer and an internet connection. These photographs capture some low-income households where the positions given to the television set tell a unique story.

With a dream of becoming a war correspondent one day, I was one of those fortunate ones who became part of the largest revolution in the Pakistani electronic media scene: the emergence of the private satellite news channels. Covering news on the frontlines for more than five leading local news channels, I witnessed the shaping of game-changing events in Pakistan. It exposed me to dangers on the frontline, like the coverage of the deadliest situations. At the same time it revealed the dangerous liaisons between the political parties and organized criminal mafias in Karachi.

Lyari unrest, Karachi
Geo English, 2007

Street agitation at Regal Chowk, Karachi
Geo English, 2007

Fire in a paint factory, Karachi
GEO English, 2008

After Benazir Bhutto's assassination, Larkana
GEO English, 2008

Politics was criminalized and crime was politicized. But the 'no news is good news' mantra has in due course of time shifted local television journalism more towards 'performing arts', which is why one now sees programme anchors encroaching the space with their 'newly acquired' walk and talk and hand signals. Advertisers on the other hand, look for and support sensational content in TV programming and thus selected programmes get the most of the advertisements, putting the real stories on the back burner.

Floods in Thatta
Aaj News, 2010

Floods in Thatta
Express News, 2011

Aftermath of 2010 floods, Sanghar
Express News, 2011

Paramilitary raid, Karachi
Express 24/7, 2011

Qasba Colony, Karachi
Express 24/7, 2011

Bureau Office, Karachi
Express 24/7, 2011

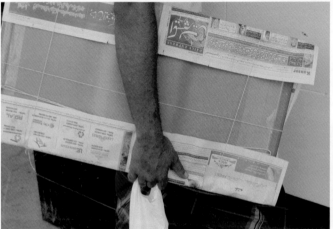

Rashid Rana

FROM RELIGIOUS AND CORPORATE ADVERTISING TO POLITICAL PROTESTS

SEEK KNOWLEEDGE ★

CAMBRIDGE MODEL SCHOOL

145

Mostly used as unofficial signage, these texts tell people they should not pee, park, photograph, loan, smoke, advertise, swim, spit or enter a public space like mosques, parks or ladies' rooms.

After the Partition, many families who migrated to Lahore from Amristar and nearby cities settled in Gawalmandi in the old city area. Over a few decades, property divisions and commercialisation drove the new generation of inhabitants to leave these family houses to move to newly developed housing schemes in Lahore's suburbs.

In the last 15 years or so, political unrest and security worries in Karachi have driven people to Lahore in an influx the likes of which has never been experienced. This has brought in money and ideas. As a result, the city has been growing along with its real estate business. These paintings are of the new homes and housing colonies that have thus sprung up across Lahore's suburbs over the last decade.

They portray the 'unfinished' façades, some blackened by tar waterproofing, that lie expectantly in wait for the next house to come up against them. This is the face of a dual geography of putting down roots and yet leaving space open for the future.

Shakil (20) male, plays 8 hours a day

Zulfiqar (15) male, plays 6 hours a day

Danish (13) male, plays 3 hours a day

Murtaza (19) male, plays 5 hours a day

Azmat (18) male, plays 4 hours a day

Aman (20) as a grown-up female, I don't get to play any more!

Patoki, Punjab

Swat Valley, Khyber Pakhtunkhwa

DIVING INTO THE UNKNOWN

While scuba diving for the last five years around Churna Island, I encountered many beautiful and delicate marine life species. The sea in the areas such as Clifton beach, Oyster Rocks, the Karachi Harbour used to be clean and clear, but was destroyed by oil spills and huge tonnes of untreated sewerage which were dumped into the sea. As a result, divers have been forced to move westwards toward Churna Island in search of cleaner water. Churna Island is also, however, under threat from a recently installed crude oil offloading floating facility and environmentally hazardous practices such as overfishing and the use of ghost nets. I fear that the areas around Churna Island will meet the same fate as the waters around Clifton.

1	Snorkel	**7**	Wetsuit (3mm)	**13**	Underwater Camera and Housing
2	Dive Mask	**8**	Integrated Weights	**14**	Alternate Air Source
3	Air Hose	**9**	BC Inflator / deflator	**15**	Dive Knife
4	Regulator	**10**	Diving Glove	**16**	Boots
5	Tank Valve	**11**	SPG (Submersible Pressure Gauge)	**17**	Adjustable Fins
6	Buoyancy Compensator (BC)	**12**	Compressed Air Tank		

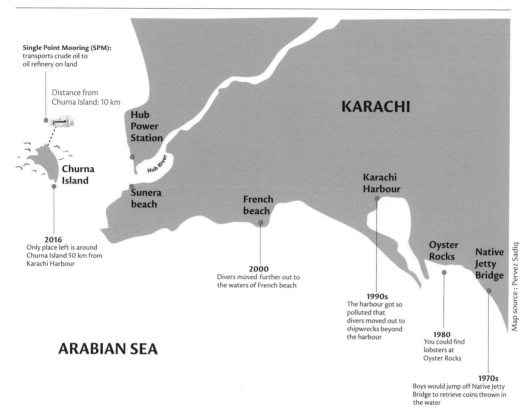

Single Point Mooring (SPM): transports crude oil to oil refinery on land

Distance from Churna Island: 10 km

KARACHI

Hub Power Station

Hub River

Churna Island

Karachi Harbour

Sunera beach

French beach

2016
Only place left is around Churna Island 50 km from Karachi Harbour

Oyster Rocks

Native Jetty Bridge

2000
Divers moved further out to the waters of French beach

1990s
The harbour got so polluted that divers moved out to shipwrecks beyond the harbour

1980
You could find lobsters at Oyster Rocks

ARABIAN SEA

Map source : Pervez Sadiq

1970s
Boys would jump off Native Jetty Bridge to retrieve coins thrown in the water

Logbook Entry Photography dive

Camera :	Sealife DC 1400
Date :	15 December 2014
Location :	Northeast Churna Island
Depth :	6 metres
Bottom time :	60 minutes
Visibility :	12 metres
Water Temperature :	27 Celcius

Marine Life Observed
Green turtle, fanworm, various fish species including wrasse, sergeant majors, ghost fishes, travelly, and species of coral, including cellular coral, finger corals, black large spine sea urchins, pillar sponge, small octopus, small pink jellyfish, binny.

In Pakistan's Sindh province, hundreds of shrines dedicated to its many Sufi saints provide ground for the province's martial art: Malakhro. A form of wrestling, the practice still holds on despite being sometimes cast aside as a rural pastime. Even in Sanskrit, *Malakhra* translates into sport wrestling as opposed to its counterpart *Malla-yuddha*, which means combat wrestling. Nevertheless, wrestlers, referred to as *pehlwans*,

Sandhra Bandhna

Sandhra Bandhna

Sandhra Khenchna

Zor Lagana

Godi Marna

Godi Marna

take the sport seriously and memorize from a young age a series of intricate moves, or *daos* that dictate pehlwans' victory or defeat. Wrestlers must play two rounds in order to ensure a victory. The one who wins the second round wins the match and is given tribute, or inam, by as many people in the crowd who offer. One wrestler may play as many as ten or twelve matches in a session of *Malakhra*, which may typically last two hours.

Uthdavan

Ghumana

Ghumana

Jhata Marna

Haath Daalna

Mal Maarna

Holi celebrations

Political rally

Cricket match

'Dhammal' — mystic dance

Concert

Navratri Prayers, Native Jetty's Sri Laxmi Narayan Mandir, Karachi

All Souls' Day, Gora Qabrustan, Karachi

9th Muharram Ziyarat, Bara Imam Bargah, Kharadar, Karachi

Razia Bibi (73)
For her son's health

Ruqayya (69)
For the return of her son from Dubai

Fatima (41)
For the elevation of her spiritual status

Amina (66)
For her deteriorating eyesight

Naima (25)
To get married

Parveen (55)
For diabetes control

The clay lamp *diya* is a symbol of hope and a way to make wishes. It is lit either in the name of elevated souls, mostly for *Panjtan Paak*, or Sufi saints as the believer supplicates them for assistance in a *mannat* or vow.

Aasia (28)
To conceive

Aalia (42)
For her daughter's marriage

**Reported to have been lit by a Sufi dervish
under an isolated tree**

Sajjida (35)
For her sister to get married

Salman (36)
For a promotion

Sajid (27)
For a job overseas

This is a photograph of a bride's *jahaiz* or *dowry*. For many families in Pakistan, a *dowry*—household goods, clothing, linen—is painstakingly scraped together and stored in a steel trunk such as this one. On the 8th of March 2013, this trunk and its contents were burnt to ashes when a mob of several thousand people attacked

over 100 homes in Lahore's Badami Bagh neighbourhood of Joseph Colony in an act of 'vigilante justice' over a blasphemy allegation. The fire destroyed everything. It is ironic that the biblical name 'Joseph' is said to have its root in the Hebrew verb for 'taken away' and 'added' or 'increased'.

A few months later, the government decided to pay all the families Rs 500,000 in compensation. Unused to being in possession of such a large sum all at once, the families decided to use it to finance weddings.

Maiyoon, first pre-wedding event

Mehndi (groom), second pre-wedding event

Mehndi (bride), third pre-wedding event

Baraat, arrival of groom on the wedding day

Indeed, after six months the fire turned into wedding season for many couples. Here are some images from that time and feature some of the key events from a Pakistani wedding ceremony.

Baraat, groom arrives at bride's place on the wedding day

Shaadi, the wedding

Valima, a reception by the groom after the wedding day

Study took our nationals to the West, and work took our people to the Middle East. While the early days of Pakistan saw many of our countrymen meeting and marrying while abroad on study, the trend has now equalised when we see numerous Pakistani women marrying partners they met locally. In many cases, these travels led to unions and additions to our society. Being the offspring of one such marriage, I thought I had a rough idea of the number of individuals residing here, but I discovered many more.

Siraj (my father), born in UP, India and Bruna (my mother), born in Verona, Italy. Married in Cambridge in 1957.

Pat-Salim (my brother), born in Dhaka (East Pakistan) and Angela, Australian of Italian immigrant parents.

Pat met Angela during his studies in Italy and got married in 1983. Both live in Melbourne now with their three children.

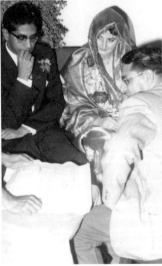

Qasim, born in Delhi, India and Helga, born in Salzburg, Austria.

Qasim met his future spouse in Salzburg. Got married in 1958 in Karachi.

Qasim & Helga (2007) Helga works as a homemaker in Islamabad.

While Pakistan could be a challenging country for many expats, most make the transition and integrate. Those who do take the plunge discover a hospitable side to its society not always apparent at first. Here is a very small sampling of couples who give Pakistani society back some of its diversity lost at Partition. There are thousands more, from virtually every continent and country represented here.

Klaus, born in Duesseldorf, Germany and Jennifer, born in Rawalpindi, Pakistan.

Klaus moved to Pakistan in 1996. Married Jennifer in Islamabad in 2000.

Klaus & Jennifer (2015) Both of them work in development in Islamabad.

Junaid, born in Rawalpindi, Pakistan & Majella Gaffney, born in Dublin, Ireland. Got married in Dublin in 1997.

Junaid and Majella (2016) Live in Islamabad where Majella works as a homemaker.

Chris (UK) and Rose (Nagar, Pakistan) married in Rawalpindi in 1995. Chris lives in Pakistan. Rose schools their adopted daugher in the UK, and connects mostly via messenger services.

SWEDEN
NORWAY
DENMARK
NETHERLANDS
GERMANY
BELGIUM
AUSTRIA
FRANCE
HUNGARY
ITALY
GREECE
TURKEY
RUSSIA
UKRAINE
KYRGYZSTAN
TAJIKISTAN
AFGHANISTAN
PAKISTAN
QUETTA
IRAN
KARACHI
SRI LANKA

● ● ● ● ● Illegal routes used by Hazaras from 2000-2014
○ Each circle represents a detention point or a change in mode of transport
● Our route to Australia

Due to decades of war in Afghanistan since the 1800s, a lot of families from our Hazara community sought asylum in Quetta, capital of Balochistan province. However, with the wave of sectarian conflict, targeted attacks, and the rise of religious groups in the past decade in Quetta, Hazaras were confined to only two localities, a 4-km radius on Alamdar Road and an 11-km area within Hazara Town, after the provincial government set up security checkpoints around our residential colonies. As a result of this situation, most of the families try to go to Europe or Australia to seek asylum. Some attempt to go as exchange students while others go through human smuggling, using illegal routes which sometimes cost them their lives. Those who survive are either deported or taken to detention centres where they continue to wait for a miracle.

MALAYSIA

INDONESIA

CHRISTMAS ISLAND
(AUSTRALIA)

AUSTRALIA

SYDNEY

PERTH

With heights of up to 7,000 m (23,000 ft), the Siachen Glacier is the highest-altitude battlefield in the world and demarcates Pakistan from India and China. The absence of any boundary line beyond the "dead end" of the Line of Control has led this region to become a contested space between India and Pakistan. As a mandatory period of military service at war-zone, I did my tenure at Siachen.

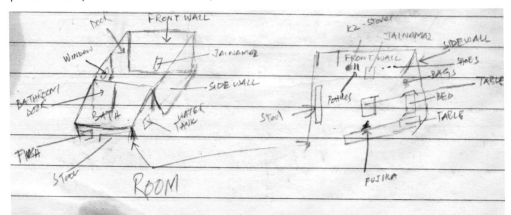

On a non-gridded mound of snow, this igloo marks a sentinel against a neighbour and the weather, both with an unknown degree of hostility. My room is a typical bunker built on self-help basis. Carved out from a hillock, it is a classical one-window room of 14x10 feet. The 10-foot high ceiling has 70 girders. Trivial information, you say? I count them every night before I could sleep. No, I have not grown insomniac, but I dare not venture out to count stars in this part of the world.*

The room décor is an artistic arrangement of the empty containers of food, fuel and fire. Food cartons serve as tables, fuel cans as stools and empty (fired) cartridges as bedside teapoy items. The most decorated table has boxes of chicken cubes, noodles, egg biscuits, brick-game and, my window to the world, the radio. There is no FM here, only the BBC and loads of incomprehensible regional channels. Other inhabitants includes a Fujika (a kerosene-lit heater), petromax, the books that you had sent and the military phone—this masterpiece of technology which connected me to you, remains silent.*

* Excerpts from my letters

In this inhospitable terrain, temprature can go as low as -40° C. Lack of communication facilities, inherent danger of weather and other hostilities merited silent deployments and conspired against any probable communication between me and my newly-wed wife. These articles offer a glimpse into how we fought the odds at our ends, how small necessities graduated to luxuries and how our relationship stood the test of time.

(1) I had to spend 90 days in the war zone. I drew a rough calendar for my wife explaining my location on any given day. It took 21 days to climb the post, 30 days to stay at the post and then one could get down and spend remaining days at a post with relatively less altitude, so the remaining days could make sense to her.

(2) Our wedding card envelope which my wife used as a letter.

(3) A demand chit for the canteen; in isolated posts, small items such as an egg, a tomato or any fresh vegetable looked like a distant dream.

(4) This was my 142nd letter. This letter came via helicopter which dropped ration items and due to height/fall effect, the things got buried in the snow and we had to dig them out. I was actually digging for chicken cubes when I found this.

(5) One of the many registers for my thoughts.

(6) In the absence of any other means of communiction, sometimes I used to record and send messages to my wife on these audio cassettes.

(7) A pillow cover used by my wife as a parcel to send books when a sturdy envelope was not available.

These letters were written by my father, Major Aslam Zuberi, to my mother, Zarina Zuberi, after the Fall of Dhaka—also referred to as the war of 1971—in which Pakistan lost its East Wing (East Pakistan). Bangladesh declared independence on December 16, 1971, with the intervention of the Indian Army. My father was among 80,000 Pakistani army personnel who surrendered, and were taken as Prisoners of War (POWs). He sent his first letter as a prisoner of war on 28 December 1971 from the Indian Field Post Office in Dhaka. The POWs were then transferred to camps in India, the locations of which remain undisclosed. The letter, dated 16 January 1972, and all the subsequent ones, came from Camp No. 54. The last letter addressed to my mother is dated 1 January, 1974. He was repatriated later that year. The exchange of these letters was facilitated by the Tracing Agency of the International Committee of the Red Cross in accordance with the Geneva Conventions.

Karachi

Camp 54

Dhaka

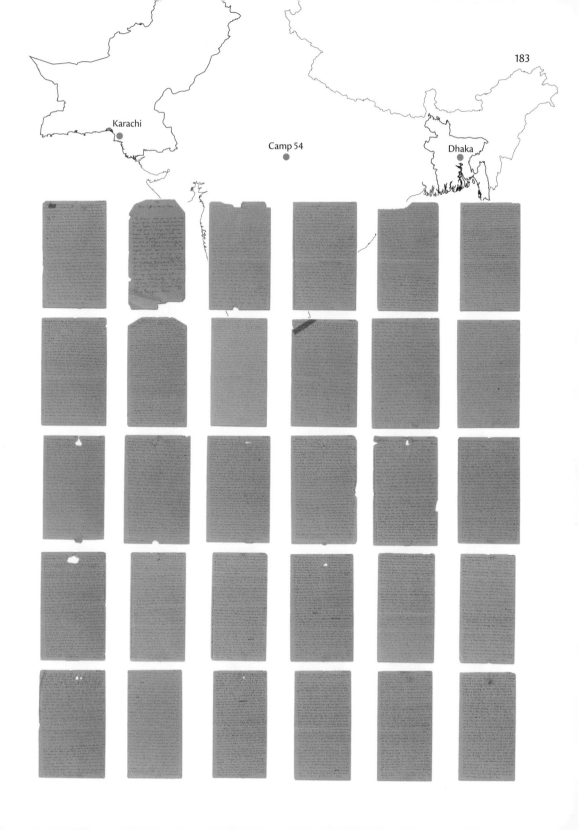

Nani Amma's journey began as an Indian. The familiar choice of migrating to East Pakistan after the partition of India in 1947 transformed her from an Indian to a Pakistani. After the split of West and East Pakistan in 1971, the whole family destroyed all their documents to avoid being seen as Biharis or immigrants from East Pakistan

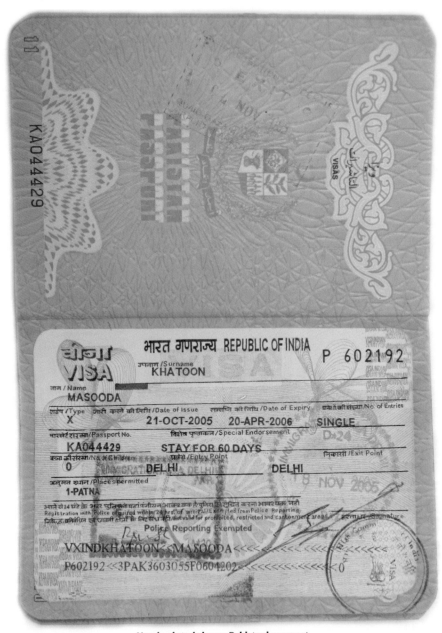

Hand painted visa on Pakistani passport
I painted this visa for India on to my grandmother's passport as a response to the numerous rejections which prevented her from visiting her home town.

(renamed Bangladesh). She tried to visit India but was declined numerous times due to her Pakistani identity. I painted an Indian visa on to her passport. Later, she acquired an American nationality because it enabled her to visit her siblings and children who had chosen to settle in the UK, India and US without any visa issues.

Lost, Burnt East Pakistani passport
Used between 1947 and 1971 after Partition and migration from India to East Pakistan

Cancelled Pakistani passport
Used between 1971 and 2009 after migrating from East Pakistan (now Bangladesh) to Pakistan

Cancelled American passport
Used between 2004 and 2013 after migrating from Pakistan to America

Renewed American passport
Using currently after migration from Pakistan to America

Partition in 1947 was the most significant event in the history of the Indian Subcontinent. An estimated 14 million people left their homes and most of them could never go back. Shafaat Hussain and Raisa Begum were one of those 14 million migrants.

Shafaat Hussain and Raisa Begum
1950, Ludhiana, Punjab, India

Shafaat Hussain and Raisa Begum
2015, Karachi, Pakistan

We are first cousins. In Ludhiana many of our relatives lived close to each other. We knew that our parents were willing to bring us together. In 1949, we got married and migrated to Pakistan. Although we want to, but for different reasons we have since been unable to visit our birthplace. And now our health doesn't permit such travel. We cannot, however, shake the memory of our birthplace where many relatives still live. We lived in a joint family system. We have memories of our family house with the green fields next to it. We used to play around the Peepal tree. We played a lot of *chuppan chupai* or hide-and-seek.

Observing maps of balkanizing Pakisan being published, and people immigrating to other countries, the attachment or detachment of patriotic ties towards any piece of land has become very strange to me.

BEGGARS

INDIAN

مہر لگائیں

PAKISTANI

مہر لگائیں

VEGETABLE SELLERS

INDIAN

مہر لگائیں

PAKISTANI

مہر لگائیں

TAILORS

PAKISTANI

مہر لگائیں

INDIAN

مہر لگائیں

Experiencing this, I have come to the conclusion that we have little control of our pasts, presents or futures. We are perhaps just goats being shepherded from one place to another.

TEA SELLERS

INDIAN

مہرلگائیں

PAKISTANI

مہرلگائیں

COBBLERS

PAKISTANI

مہرلگائیں

INDIAN

مہرلگائیں

POLICEMEN

PAKISTANI

مہرلگائیں

INDIAN

مہرلگائیں

Wagah/Atari border performs a daily ritual around sunset that is witnessed by thousands of patriotics on both sides of the Pakistan-India border. Pakistani Rangers show off their rehearsed performance in which their moves are well-coordinated with the Indian soldiers. They celebrate the ritual of separation while lowering the flags and closing the border for the day,

which reopens the next morning for people to cross migrate. The ritual is highly seductive; both soldiers are continuously trying to outdo each other. In this series of paintings, the background and the physical presence of the border has been removed to highlight the tension and play of power.

These permutations and combinations of national badges, a symbol of identity, produced by mixed cultural practices, represent a strange and obscure objects-of-desire map of Pakistani culture. From a Tweety Bird holding a Pakistani flag or Mickey Mouse dressed in Pakistani green or a small green flag, there are no pure forms of national representations.

Everything is hybridized or a result of convergence of several, and at times even competing and conflicting, national, global and cultural traditions. As class system, force, power and coercion continue to determine the choice of product(s) of identity, we continue to struggle to maintain and preserve the particularities of our national identity.

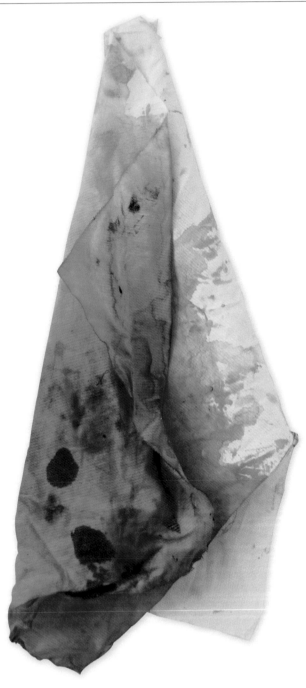

USed
Ikram Mengal

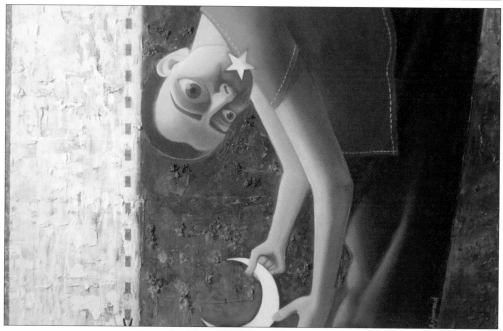

I am flexible, are you?
Sana Arjumand

Watering the land of the pure
Sana Arjumand

The cut
Zulfikar Ali Bhutto

Grass was greener
Areej Fatima

Pakistan today
RM Naeem

...and there was light!
Ibrahim Yahya

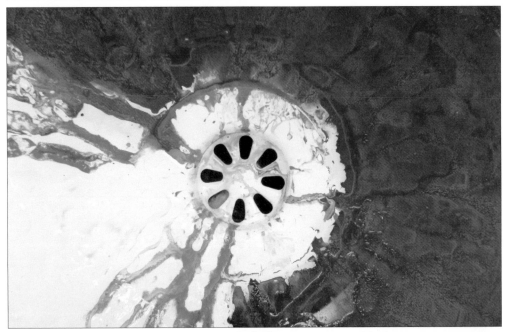

Drained
Samar Raza

Entangled
Sara Khan

Minority report
Haseebullah Ahmadzad

It's not that far
Shafaq Afzal

Quick fix
Hazique Zaheer

Making room
Qasim Naeem

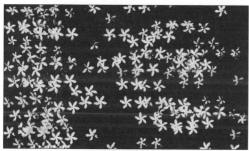

Of the same garden
Roohi Ahmed

PakUStan
Maham Bosan

A white star and a crescent on a dark green field, with a verticle white stripe at the hoist.According to the specifications it is a dark green rectangular flag in the proportion of length [A] and width [B] as 3:2 with a white vertical bar at the mast, the green portion bearing a white crescent in the centre and a five-pointed white heraldic star. The width of the white portion [C] is one quarter the width of the flag [A], nearest the mast, so the green portion occupies the remaining three quarters [D].Draw a diagonal L3 from the top right hand corner to the bottom left corner of the green portion. On this diagonal establish two points P1 and P2. P1 is positioned at the centre of the green portion and P2 at the intersection of the diagonal L3 and an arc C4 created from the top right hand corner equal to 13/20 the height of the flag [B]. With the centre at point P1 and a radius 9/10 the height of the flag describe the first circle C1 and with centre at point P2 and a radius 11/40 the height of the flag describe a second circle C2. The enclosures made by these two circles form the crescent. The dimensions of the five-pointed white heraldic star are determined by drawing a circle C3 with a radius 1/10 the height of the flag positioned between P2 and P3 on the diagonal L3. The circle surrounds the five points of the heraldic star and star lies with one point on the diagonal L3 at point P3 where the

Wikistan
Rabeya Jalil

Kingdom of Pakistan
Samar Raza

In the name of God
Shumyl Haider

Watch out!
Sarah Javed

The fall
Maham Bosan

Everyone thinks about themselves
Saira Zia

Reaching out!
Zainab Marvi

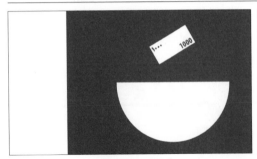

Let's start!
Ibrahim Yahya

Bravery in blood
Saadia Abdul Rashid

Teatime, any time!
Ruhy Nasir

Connecting people
Ruhy Nasir

Nuclear Pakistan
Khadeeja Raza

Cornered
Areesha Channah

Positive Pakistan
Saadia Abdul Rashid

The centralized
Uroos Nazim

Zinda bhaag
Faran Haider

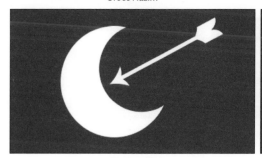

Targeted
Areej Fatima

Recycling nation
Sarah Javed

Adeela Suleman
(1970, Karachi)
Visual artist
p. 192-193

Ahmed Ali Manganhar
(1974, Tando Allahyar)
Visual artist
p. 92-93

Ahsan Jamal
(1975, Jhang)
Visual artist
p. 25, 188-189

Aleem Dad Khan
(1980, Karimabad, Hunza)
Visual artist
p. 52-53

Alyna Farooqi
(1991, Karachi)
Artist, writer
p. 140-141

Aman Asif
(1994, Lahore)
Art student
p. 154-155

Ambreen Shahwani
(1996, Quetta)
Art student
p. 25

Annelys De Vet
(1974, Alkmaar, NL)
Designer, initiator
p. 6-7

Anousha Tehseen
(1993, Karachi)
Graphic designer
p. 26

Areej Fatima
(1993, Karachi)
Graphic designer
p. 196, 201

Areesha Channah
(1993, Karachi)
Graphic designer
p. 201

Arsalan Hanif
(1995, Karachi)
Graphic designer
p. 26, 122-123, 124-125

Arif Mahmood
(1960, Karachi)
Photographer
p. 166-169

Ayaz Jokhio
(1978, Mehrabpur)
Visual artist
p. 16-17, 18

Chandan Baloch
(1997, Turbat)
Art student
p. 18

Danial Shah
(1989, Quetta)
Travel photographer
p. 46-47

Durriya Kazi
(1955, Karachi)
Visual artist, educator
p. 34-35, 120-121

Faran Haider
(1990, Lahore)
Communication designer
p. 201

Farooq Soomro
(1980, Sukkur)
Photographer, writer
p. 60-63

Farrukh Afaq
(1993, Karachi)
Graphic designer
p. 26, 96-97